VOICES INTERNATIONAL PUBLICATIONS
PRESENTS

HOW TO NAVIGATE THROUGH FEDERAL PRISON AND GAIN AN EARLY RELEASE

WRITTEN BY

LISA BARRETT

WITH JAMILA T. DAVIS

How to Navigate Through Federal Prison And Gain An Early Release

Copyright © 2015 by Lisa Barrett

All rights reserved. This book or any portion thereof may not be reproduced or used in any manner whatsoever without the express written permission of the publisher, except for the use of brief quotations in a book review.

Disclaimer
This book is written to enlighten readers about the basic functions, policies and structure of Federal Prison Camps and low-security Federal Correctional Institutions. All information enclosed was derived from the author's personal experience, research and interviews with inmates behind bars. Experiences of prisoners may differ based on their circumstances and the facilities where they are housed. Therefore, some examples may not apply to all prisoners. This book is written to be a companion to federal inmates to provide basic information about their journey through imprisonment and to expose common pitfalls. It is not written to provide professional legal advice or counseling. Readers who are seeking legal advice, are urged to consult a criminal defense attorney or professional prison consultant.

Printing in the United States of America
First Printing, 2015

Library of Congress Control Number: 2014921581
ISBN: 978-0-9911041-4-7

Voices International Publications
196-03 Linden Boulevard
St. Albans, NY 11412
"Changing Lives a Page at a Time."
www.voicebooks.com

Typesetting by: Jade Rade www.impactstudioonline.com
Cover Design by: Marion Designs www.mariondesigns.com
Edited by: Jamila T. Davis and Catherine Floyd

ACKNOWLEDGMENTS

To Jamila Davis, I humbly offer my gratitude for making this project possible. This book would still be just an idea without you! You are a woman with more energy, enthusiasm and spirit than anyone I've ever known. You empower those around you to be more than they believe they could ever be and I thank you for that.

To Catherine Floyd, thanks for your input, patience and strong beliefs. You inspire confidence in all of us.

To my crazy, big family - Aunt Dora, Lori, Cathy, Terri, Chuck, Gary, Mark, Kevin and their spouses, Mike, Tommy, AnnMarie, Maria, Ann Marie and Michelle for standing with me through good and bad times and for making the weekly treks to Connecticut for nine months, even though I know Cathy bullied all of you. We can laugh at just about anything - even this!

To JD, my only child, my pride and joy! The one person who has had to bear the biggest burden of my incarceration. I admire your strength and perseverance. I love you the best, the most, always and forever!

To my BFF, Debbie, thank you for being my friend through everything. You never wavered or gave up on me, even when I gave up on myself and you made me believe I could actually write a book!

For the input of Renese, Patti, Carrie, Janel, Barb and Dorian, I am so grateful. You willingly shared your unique journeys through the Federal prison system, making this book more poignant and personal.

I extend my gratitude to the women of Danbury FPC (you know who you are) for caring for each other every day like family would. You are now part of my extended family.

Finally, a big shout out to "C" Dorm - the coolest ladies I know, especially to my precious South Philly bunkie, Elizabeth and my "gangsta" New York bunkie, Carmen, who always made me laugh through the tears.

HOW TO NAVIGATE THROUGH FEDERAL PRISON AND GAIN AN EARLY RELEASE

TABLE OF CONTENTS

Introduction 7
Chapter One - Changing Your Perspective:
  Prison Isn't As Bad As You Think 11
Chapter Two - Prison Crash Course 101: Understanding
  The Basics Of The Bureau Of Prisons (BOP) 17
Chapter Three - Day 1:
  Starting The Prison Journey. 26
Chapter Four - Day 2:
  Getting Acquainted With Prison Life And Knowing
  What To Expect. 36
Chapter Five - Admissions & Orientation (A&O):
  Learning The Basic Rules & Regulations 46
Chapter Six - Mail, Telephone, Email:
  Staying Connected With The Outside World. 64
Chapter Seven - Commissary And Prison Meals:
  Buying What You Need And Eating
  To Survive In Prison 78
Chapter Eight - Prison Politics 101:
  Prison Work Assignments And Duties 92
Chapter Nine - Leisure Time And Recreational Activities:
  Making The Best Out Of Time! 100
Chapter Ten - Prison Programs And Services:
  Knowing What The BOP Has To Offer. 110
Chapter Eleven - Legal Remedies From Behind Bars:
  Justice For Inmates! 126
Chapter Twelve - Federal Prison from A Woman's Perspective:
  Female Offenders Questions & Answers (Q&A) 140

Chapter Thirteen - Transfers, Furloughs And Methods
  To Gain A Speedy Release: The Beginning of the End! 160
Afterword... 175
Bibliography 177
Glossary 181
Resources.. 193
Index 207

INTRODUCTION

It happened after work on a brisk, winter day in January of 2013 and I will never forget it. My schedule included attending my son's hockey game that night, organizing his church youth group gathering the next day and attending a Super Bowl party on Sunday. Basking in gratitude to the universe, I started my day by giving thanks for being happy, healthy and alive. Life had thrown me some intense curve balls. In my 47 years of life, I faced divorce and the death of both my parents, yet I managed to land on my feet. I thought being diagnosed with breast cancer in 2011 was sure to have been the most frightening battle of my life. After 16 weeks of chemotherapy treatments to fight this deadly disease, I had lost a significant amount of my strength and every follicle of hair on my head, but I was now healthy. Although life's punches were tough I was determined to stay strong and fight fervently to overcome, just as I had coached my students for the past 27 years teaching in the public school system of Northeastern Pennsylvania. Ending the long, fierce battle, it seemed as though I had finally triumphed over all my obstacles. The cancer was gone and I was ready to start the next chapter of my life with new meaning. Engaged to the man with whom I believed to be the love of my life, our wedding was scheduled for March 2nd, less than two months away. My plans were to travel the world and live the life of my dreams. Things couldn't be better, or so I thought.

"Knock, knock!" I heard a pounding on my door as the door bell loudly rang. I wasn't expecting guests, so the pounding startled me. Opening the door, I was faced by two male federal agents. "Good afternoon, are you Lisa Barrett?" Something inside me said that this one visit would change the course of my life and it has!

One year later, in January, 2014, I stood before the Honorable James Munley in the Middle District Court of Pennsylvania. After pleading guilty to embezzlement and theft of labor union funds, the judge handed me a one-year sentence, but not before giving me a lecture on how I was too intelligent to have ended up in his courtroom. On top of managing my home and my classroom, I also managed my local teacher's union, serving as President for six years. As a Board member of the state Political Action Committee for Education (PACE), I was a strong advocate for quality public education, which is often underfunded. Having traveled the state of Pennsylvania lobbying and talking to key legislators to create positive change for public education and teacher's rights, I had become well known. In my mind, I could do it all, but at some point it all became overwhelming. Through mismanagement of union funds, money was spent on items I was not authorized to purchase. This mistake led to the imposition of a one year prison sentence, $59,273 in restitution and two years probation.

Standing frozen as the judge continued to lecture and explain how he was tired of reading about "people like me" in the newspaper every day, reality settled in. I was stunned and couldn't believe I was going to prison. How would I survive? Then I heard the muffled cries from behind me in the courtroom where my family and friends were seated. Being the cause of their pain sent me over the edge. I joined them bellowing sobs of grief. I held tightly on to the arm of my attorney so when my knees gave out, I wouldn't hit the floor. Now I had to get myself together to face the onslaught of the press that awaited me outside. At that very moment, I didn't think life could get any worse. In my mind, death would have been better than prison.

This story is being shared with you because our experiences may be similar. I'm writing this book from the top bunk in a cubicle at Danbury Federal Prison Camp in Danbury, Connecticut. It's almost a year later and I am winding down to the end of my sentence. What I once felt was impossible to overcome, is almost behind me. After all of this, I know for sure I can face any obstacle that comes my way!

As a life long educator, I felt it was important to create a book for people like myself who have no clue what to expect after being sentenced to federal prison. Shortly after my sentencing, I paid a $5,000 fee to a prison consultant to help me navigate through the federal prison system. Although the information he gave me was helpful, I felt there were important parts missing. He had never been incarcerated and could not give me all the detailed information from the perspective of an inmate to ease my adjustment to prison life.

INTRODUCTION

"How to Navigate Through Federal Prison and Gain an Early Release" is written to give the reader a solid overview of the functions of the Bureau of Prisons (BOP) and prepare you on what to expect. It is my goal to equip you with the basic rules and functions of a federal prison. I gained valuable insight from some incredible women who have assisted me in completing this project. Sharing my personal experiences along with theirs will provide you with useful pointers on how to survive in prison and get out as quickly as possible. Although I was sentenced to a year, which would not have given me any 'good time' days at all, I managed to gain a release date three months prior to my scheduled date. I was blessed to meet some seasoned inmates who taught me the ropes.

This guide is filled with all the valuable information which would have been great to have known prior to my incarceration. It is my hope it will empower you with the art of survival in prison and become your compass to help navigate the many twists and turns new prisoners face.

Prison is not the end of the world, as I once thought. It is a place where many, including myself, have found opportunities to do intense soul searching and create plans and alliances for a successful future. You may be saying to yourself, "Yeah, right!" But, what I am sharing is all real. Not only will you become an informed inmate - the one who knows what to expect, what to bring, how to communicate with the outside world, and how to gain an early release, I'll also teach you how to make the best out of your time.

Remember this journey is only temporary. As my friend Jill says, "You'll get to the other side and this will all be a thing of the past." The only way to get through is to go through. The good thing is you are not alone. Let's navigate this journey together and come out on top!

Chapter 1
Changing Your Perspective

Prison Isn't as Bad as You Think!

So, you've been sentenced to serve time in federal prison. If you are anything like I once was, you may be thinking this is the worst thing that could ever happen to you. Let me assure you this doesn't have to be the case! What I discovered behind bars is nothing I would have ever imagined. I've met some incredible people who happened to have made a mistake, just like I did. Through this experience, we've gotten to spend extensive hours with each other, creating new relationships. Separated from our families, we've become each others' protectors and allies. We turn to one another for moral support and comfort in times of despair.

I've had the unique opportunity to meet women of all backgrounds, ethnicities and social classes. I've learned many valuable life lessons from them. I thought I'd simply be trying to race through my prison time as fast as I could, never to look back, but my heart led me to have compassion for the women with whom I was housed. Part of that compassion developed when I realized the lengthy sentences many of them were serving for non-violent crimes as first time offenders. I came to learn of the huge sentencing disparities between male and female white collar offenders from a study completed by CultureQuantiX based on 29 women housed at Danbury Federal Prison Camp. It revealed that the women received 300% greater sentences than their male counterparts who were convicted of the same or similar crimes. The number was 480% amongst African American women. (See WomenOverIncarcerated.org) I was appalled! I felt obligated to do something after I learned of the severe injustices within the U.S. judicial system.

As I explained in my introduction, I was once the President of my local teachers' union. I defended teacher's rights and was trained to lobby and advocate for public education. Now, I feel compelled to do the same for women behind bars.

This book is being written to create a much overdue, detailed, functional resource for those who may be frightened and do not know what to expect in prison. Having experienced the same pain, it is my desire to use my insight to help others. With a $59,273 loss amount in a white collar case, I felt I should have been sentenced to probation. For some time, I questioned why I had to take this journey through prison. Today, I understand it was all in God's plan.

My life has changed immensely, and I now recognize there was purpose for my hardship. While incarcerated, I had the opportunity to do some real soul searching as well as a chance to devise an incredible plan for my life moving forward. With that being said, what seemed to be the end of the road turned out not to be so bad. A lot of women who once felt like I did in the beginning, now have had a change of heart based on experience. Chances are, you will feel the same way too!

I will now introduce you to a phenomenal woman who has helped me significantly on this phase of my journey so you can get her perspective on imprisonment. I believe her story will further help to change your outlook.

TURNING MY LEMONS INTO LEMONADE
by: Jamila T. Davis

On July 16, 2008, I was sentenced before Honorable Jose Linares in the District Court of New Jersey. I was convicted of seven counts of bank fraud and ordered to serve 12 1/2 years in federal prison. Life as I knew it was over, or so I thought. I had no clue how I would be able to serve such a lengthy sentence.

I am not suggesting it has been easy, however, to date I've served over 6 1/2 years behind bars. Although, what I am about to say may sound strange, I quickly realized there was great purpose for my incarceration. Behind bars, I embarked upon an intense journey of inner healing and self-discovery. For many years I equated success and self-worth with status and wealth. I believed the more you had, the better off you were. Therefore my entire adult life was consumed with what I call "chasing." I chased after people, places and things, as I climbed to even greater heights of success. As a Celebrity Advisor and real estate investor, I became a self-made multimillionaire by the age of 25. A few careless choices led to the end of my reign on top. By the age of 31, I was sent to the Danbury Federal Correctional Institution to serve a decade plus sentence behind bars.

Stripped away from all my material possessions and separated from my children, family and friends, I began to back track the steps that contributed to my downfall. The hardest part was admitting my mistakes. I wanted to blame everyone except myself. No longer able to hide my deficiencies, I had to take off my mask and reveal my true vulnerabilities. As I fought my way through denial, I emerged empowered. This opened the door for me to heal, accept responsibility and figure out how to make the most of my situation.

The average person would think with a sentence like mine there could be no hope, but I learned how to defy the odds. By developing a stronger relationship with God, I was able to surrender. As I prayed for God to lead me and reveal His plan for my incarceration, I made amazing discoveries. Instead of looking at myself as a victim, I began to envision myself as a victor. I intensely studied all of the women around me and took note of resources we all were missing. There are limited programs in prisons, so hurting women cling to each other, sometimes creating destructive relationships. Consequently, chaos and turmoil are the result. This is a sad but true reality. It became my desire to help incarcerated women heal, recognize their potential and recapture their dreams.

With the help of my family members and friends, I created the "Voice of Consequences Enrichment Series." This three book non-denominational, faith based series has helped foster real rehabilitation for incarcerated women throughout the U.S. I've gained no greater pleasure than to read the testimonies of women who have said my books have substantially helped them.

Recognizing the power I possessed through my writing, I also created "The High Price I Had to Pay" book series, which gives incarcerated women a platform to tell their stories and expose the injustices we faced within the U.S. judicial system. Our books have been nominated for notable awards and used as educational tools to deter at risk youth throughout the nation from committing crimes. Additionally, the books sparked the creation of the WomenOverIncarcerated.org advocacy group, which was formed to shed light on the lengthy sentences women face within the U.S. judicial system and to rally for sentencing reform.

From behind bars, I was able to take the lemons I was served and turn them into lemonade. Today, I am a successful author, a co-founder of a non-profit organization and a college graduate, all accomplished during my incarceration. It is not my suggestion that everyone will be as productive, but it is possible; I'm a living example.

Of course, I wish I didn't have to experience such a painful ordeal, but I've learned many valuable lessons. Having my freedom snatched away made me re-evaluate the things in life that really count.

I realized through my experiences that God allows obstacles to occur to change our course in life. I've seen incredible miracles occur from behind bars. Broken families have been reunited, women have gained the strength to quit bad drug habits, women have united in the free world and formed powerful partnerships. They've continued their education and gained powerful contacts.

In the free world I was so caught up in the "chase" I often failed to spend quality time with my family. I was always just way too busy. It wasn't until I hit a brick wall and was abandoned by my peers that I realized how valuable family can truly be. When all others scatter, your family may be your main line of support. Today, I value the hours I get to spend with my family in the prison visiting room. I look forward to smiling at my Dad and holding my daughter's hands tightly. I can't wait to get out of prison and shower my love and affection upon them.

Truthfully, I have a whole new outlook on life and I'm sure you will too! One thing for certain is you will be able to see who is real and who is fake. When the smoke clears, it may be painful to see the results, yet it will be most helpful. Knowing who you can truly depend on in life will help you build a strong support team and add value to your significant relationships.

My advice to you is to put away the Kleenex tissues and stop feeling sorry for yourself. You made a mistake, but it's not the end of the world! Program your mind to see what good can come out of this situation and focus on that. Whatever you label your experience, you set the tone for the outcome. Therefore, stop pronouncing doom upon the journey you are about to take. Instead be open, surrender and explore. Use your time behind bars to do some inner work that can be useful for the rest of your life. Reach out to your "Higher Power" and seek spiritual growth. You are way stronger than you can imagine! Not everything behind bars is bad. Look for the good and you'll find interesting people whom you can learn from. During my prison stay I've met Grammy Award winners, Senators, lawyers, doctors, tycoons and PHD's who've taught me a lot. I've even learned valuable lessons from people from the street. Each day I seek out the good and it finds me. I realize that although the government has the ability to lock up my body, no one can lock up my mind. I am confined, yet I am free to be me and I will prosper no matter where my journey leads. You can do the same!

God's Greatest Blessings,
Jamila T. Davis
www.jamiladavis.com

Chapter 2

Prison Crash Course 101

Understanding The Basics Of The Bureau Of Prisons (BOP)

HISTORY

The Bureau of Prisons (BOP) was established in 1930. It is a division of the U.S. Department of Justice that is responsible for the administration of the federal prison system. The BOP consists of more than 120 institutions, seven regional offices, its headquarters in Washington, DC, two staff training centers and 26 community corrections offices. It is also responsible for the custody and care of approximately 210,000 federal offenders and employs over 38,000 staff members.

When federal offenders are sentenced to serve time in prison, their cases are referred to the BOP, which processes the files and assigns these individuals to one of the prisons within their federal prison system. Offenders are designated based on the information provided in their Pre-Sentence Report (PSR), which is prepared by the U.S. Probation Department prior to sentencing.

SECURITY LEVELS AND DESIGNATION

The information contained in your PSR is crucial, as it is heavily relied upon by the Judge, the BOP, U.S. Probation, and the staff at federal prisons. After analyzing the PSR of each offender, the Designation and Sentence Computation Center (DSCC) located in Grand Prairie, Texas designates the offender to a specific prison and performs a sentence computation that calculates the time each individual will serve cumulating with what will be their anticipated release date. This calculation is based on the statutory "good time" accumulated by inmates and includes lump sum extra "good time" awards. Currently all federal inmates are eligible to receive 15% credit for good time if they are serving sentences greater than one year. For instance, a year and a day sentence would allow an inmate to receive 54 days off their sentence for Good Conduct Time (GCT). Therefore, on a year and a day sentence an offender would serve approximately ten months. It is important to note there is no parole for Federal sentences after November 1, 1987.

Based on the information provided in an offender's PSR and his or her sentence computation, the individual will be classified into one of five security levels - minimum, low, medium, high or administrative. These classifications are determined by the level of security and staff supervision that the individual will require to maintain safety within the institution and is based on his or her security score calculated by the DSCC. The BOP's SENTRY computer database calculates a point score that directly affects the inmate's custody level. The SENTRY system takes into account a variety of factors including: voluntary surrender eligibility, severity of offense, criminal history score documented in the PSR, history of violence/prior escape attempts, detainers (charges pending or an immigration hold), age, education and substance abuse history. In addition, the DSCC takes into account Public Safety Factors (PSF) when determining security levels. Consequently, inmates with longer sentences, a history of gang affiliation, violent behavior or sex offenders receive higher points, resulting in a higher security level.

MINIMUM SECURITY inmates include men who have 0-11 points and women who have 0 - 15 points. These individuals are typically housed at Federal Prison Camps (FPCs), which have dormitory style housing, a relatively low staff to inmate ratio, no fences and very little violence. Most inmates in FPCs, who are also known as "Campers," are low level drug dealers and white collar criminals who require minimum security. These institutions are work and program oriented and usually located adjacent to a larger prison or military base where inmates serve the labor needs of the prison or base.

LOW SECURITY inmates include men who have 12-15 points or women who have 16-30 points. These individuals are typically housed at low-security Federal Correctional Institutions (FCI Low), which have double-fenced perimeters, mostly dormitory housing and strong work and program components. At an FCI, there is a greater staff to inmate ratio to maintain the security of the institution. Inmates in these institutions pose a greater security risk than "Campers."

MEDIUM SECURITY inmates include men who have 16-23 points. These individuals are typically housed at medium security Federal Correctional Institutions (FCI Medium), which have strengthened perimeters that generally include double fences plus electronic detection systems. An FCI Medium also includes cell-type housing, a variety of work and treatment programs and an even higher staff to inmate ratio than low security institutions, ultimately providing greater internal controls.

HIGH SECURITY inmates include men who have 24+ points and women who have 31+ points. These individuals are typically housed at high-security institutions, also known as United States Penitentiaries (USPs), which have highly secured perimeters (including walled or double fences), multiple and single occupant cell housing, close staff supervision and movement controls.

The higher the security level, the more restraints initially placed on the inmate. Yet, the BOP allows inmates to reduce their point level over time by staying clear of disciplinary actions and by participating in programs. Additionally, the BOP, at any time, can place a Management Variable (MGTV) on an individual as the Bureau sees fit, which will allow the individual to be placed in a higher security facility regardless of the points the individual has.

After the DSCC determines the security level of an inmate, the individual is designated to a facility that matches the inmates custody level. Generally, the inmate is designated as close to home as possible. In certain instances, if bed space is not available, offenders may be designated to a facility outside their home region. In this instance, after serving at least a year in the designated institution, the inmate is eligible to apply for a transfer to a facility closer to home.

PRISON STAFF

It is important that you familiarize yourself with the terminology of prison staff members as you will need to call upon them for various reasons. Below you will find a list of their titles and functions:

It is vital that all inmates follow the chain of command. The BOP is a massive Federal bureaucracy. Therefore, all requests must be filed on appropriate Bureau provided forms, with the appropriate official. The most general form used is a Cop Out, also known as a BP-A148. This form is used to make any request to a member of the prison staff.

ASSOCIATE WARDEN (AW) - The individual who assists the Warden with day to day duties ensuring the security of the institution. In larger facilities there may be more than one AW.

CAPTAIN - The individual in charge of all prison guards who supervises and maintains control over the security of the institution.

CORRECTIONAL OFFICER (CO) - refers to the prison guards or officers who guard the prison facility. They are usually dressed in white or blue shirts with their names embroidered on the left side and blue khaki pants. These individuals can be called upon if you have security issues or general questions about the function of the facility.

LIEUTENANT (LT) - A higher ranking CO who supervises prison guards. If a problem occurs that the assigned prison guard is unable to handle, inmates can request to see the LT in charge. When an inmate is causing a problem, the CO will frequently call for a LT to oversee disciplinary actions.

UNIT CASE MANAGER - (See Case Manager) The staff person responsible for all casework services and other documentation relating to an inmate's commitment such as classification material, progress reports, release plans, transfers, Financial Responsibility Program payments. The Unit Case Manager serves as a liaison with the administration, Residential Re-entry Center personnel and criminal justice authorities. The Case

Manager conducts team meetings where an inmate is supplied release information and is assisted with plans for release.

UNIT COUNSELOR - (See Counselor) The staff person who provides counseling and guidance for inmates in terms of adjusting to prison. He or she is the individual to approach with personal difficulties. The Unit Counselor regularly assists in resolving day to day problems, approves visitors and assists with attorney calls. He or she is typically the first person you will meet during intake and will assist you with your telephone and email set up.

UNIT MANAGER/CAMP ADMINISTRATOR - The staff person responsible for security and general operations of a unit or Camp. He or she is responsible for planning, developing, implementing, supervising and coordinating individual programs tailored to meet the particular needs of inmates in his or her unit. In addition, the Unit Manager generally supervises the Unit Counselor and Unit Case Manager. Therefore, he or she can be sought out to rectify problems inmates have with these individuals. In FPCs the Unit Manager is referred to as the Camp Administrator.

WARDEN - The individual who holds the highest position over all institution staff and oversees the operation of the entire institution. He or she must sign off on all major decisions rendered throughout the institution.

All requests do not have to be in writing. Administrative staff are generally available daily during main line lunch. Prison staff, including high ranking officials, stand in the Dining Hall in view of the inmates to make themselves available for questions or inmate concerns. In addition, Case Managers and Counselors have open house hours, which are generally displayed on their office door. Keep in mind, you may rather utilize a Cop Out so you will have a written response to your question or concern. It may be needed to file a future grievance through the administrative remedy process, which we will discuss further along in this book.

KEY TERMS AND DEFINITIONS:

ASSOCIATE WARDEN (AW) - The individual who assists the Warden with day to day duties ensuring the security of the institution. In larger facilities there may be more than one AW.

BUREAU OF PRISONS (BOP) - A division of the U.S. Department of Justice responsible for the administration of the Federal prison system.

CAPTAIN - The individual in charge of all prison guards who supervises and maintains control over the security of the institution.

COP OUT - The form completed by an inmate to make a request of staff. Officially called a BPA-148

CORRECTIONAL OFFICER (CO) - refers to the prison guards or officers who guard the prison facility. They are usually dressed in white or blue shirts with their names embroidered on the left side and blue khaki pants. These individuals can be called upon if you have security issues or general questions about the function of the facility.

DESIGNATION AND SENTENCE COMPUTATION CENTER (DSCC) - A division of the BOP, located in Grand Prairie, Texas that designates offenders to a specific prison and performs sentence computation to calculate sentence length and release date.

GOOD CONDUCT TIME (GCT) - The amount of time credited to an inmate for sentences over one year.

JUDGMENT AND COMMITMENT ORDER (J&C) - The J&C is also referred to as the Judgment Order or Judgment. It is the court-issued document that stipulates the duration of the sentence, monetary penalty amount, if any, and conditions of release. A copy of the J&C may be obtained from the Case Manager.

LIEUTENANT (LT) - A higher ranking CO who supervises prison guards. If a problem occurs that the assigned prison guard is unable to handle, inmates can request to see the LT in charge. When an inmate is causing a problem, the CO will frequently call for a LT to oversee disciplinary actions.

MANAGEMENT VARIABLE (MGTV) - A variable used in determining inmate placement in higher security Federal facilities regardless of the points the individual has.

CHAPTER 2: UNDERSTANDING THE BASICS OF THE BUREAU OF PRISONS (BOP)

PRE-SENTENCE REPORT (PSR) - Also known as the Pre-Sentence Investigative Report (PSI). A report prepared by the U.S. Probation Department prior to an offender's sentencing that includes personal history and the details of the offense committed, among other important information. The PSR is heavily utilized by the Judge, BOP, U.S. Probation and prison staff.

SENTRY - The BOP computer database that keeps track of information about the security level of inmates, which directly affects the offender's custody level based on a variety of factors including: voluntary surrender eligibility, severity of offense, criminal history score, history of violence or escape attempts, detainers, age, education and substance abuse history.

UNIT CASE MANAGER - (See Case Manager) The staff person responsible for all casework services and other documentation relating to an inmate's commitment such as classification material, progress reports, release plans, transfers, Financial Responsibility Program payments. The Unit Case Manager serves as a liaison with the administration, Residential Re-entry Center personnel and criminal justice authorities. The Case Manager conducts team meetings where an inmate is supplied release information and is assisted with plans for release.

UNIT COUNSELOR - (See Counselor) The staff person who provides counseling and guidance for inmates in terms of adjusting to prison. He or she is the individual to approach with personal difficulties. The Unit Counselor regularly assists in resolving day to day problems, approves visitors and assists with attorney calls. He or she is typically the first person you will meet during intake and will assist you with your telephone and email set up.

UNIT MANAGER/CAMP ADMINISTRATOR - The staff person responsible for security and general operations of a unit or Camp. He or she is responsible for planning, developing, implementing, supervising and coordinating individual programs tailored to meet the particular needs of inmates in his or her unit. In addition, the Unit Manager generally supervises the Unit Counselor and Unit Case Manager. Therefore, he or she can be sought out to rectify problems inmates have with these individuals. In FPCs the Unit Manager is referred to as the Camp Administrator.

WARDEN - The individual who holds the highest position over all institution staff and oversees the operation of the entire institution. He or she must sign off on all major decisions rendered throughout the institution.

Chapter 3
Day 1

Starting The Prison Journey

The dreaded day swiftly approached, as much as I wished it hadn't—Thursday, March 27, 2014. I was scheduled to report to Danbury Federal Prison Camp (FPC) in Danbury Connecticut. For months I toiled in grief, fearing the unknown. Just when I thought things couldn't get any worse, I hit another bump in the road prior to my incarceration. Originally I was scheduled to report on March 5, 2014, but due to an error I was designated to a medical facility in Carswell Texas. Immediately I panicked, with the thought of being sent over 1,000 miles from my home in Pennsylvania. I knew I needed to act fast, so I hired a well known prison advocate, also known as prison consultant, who instructed my lawyer to request an extension from my sentencing judge. Luckily that request was granted, which gave the advocate time to handle the matter.

With help from the consultant, I quickly became enlightened to the BOP's procedures for prison admittance. It turned out that they determined I was sick based on my previous breast cancer diagnosis. By this point, I had fully recovered, which was unknown to the BOP. My advocate was able to fax my updated medical records and I was re-designated to Danbury FPC just before my extension was about to expire. In addition to assisting with my re-designation and as part of his consultation, the advocate facilitated communication with a woman who had recently been released from the same prison Camp I would now be entering. The woman gave me a run down of what to expect and provided names of inmates whom I should ask for upon my arrival. Hearing her words of reassurance that the place I was headed to was like a summer Camp, where I could work out, rest and get manicures and pedicures gave me a great sense of relief. After speaking to her, for the first time, I felt I was going to endure what was ahead of me. The comfort of knowing what to expect and my re-designation cost me a hefty fee of $5,000, but I felt it was well worth it. Although I still dreaded having to go to prison, after this ordeal, I was grateful to be housed close to my family and friends and I was mentally prepared for what was ahead.

Instructed by my consultant to report to prison between 9:00am - 11:00am to avoid being placed in the Special Housing Unit (SHU), I was up early on the morning of March 27th. The consultant told me the SHU, which is often referred to as the "hole" is an undesirable, segregated part of the prison where inmates serve time on disciplinary sanctions. When new admittances arrive too late and the staff does not have time to fully process them, they are housed in the SHU and sometimes forgotten until a staff member has time to properly intake them. This experience has been labeled as horrifying by many inmates that have endured the process, so I was advised to avoid it at all costs.

The night before I departed I said my goodbyes to my 14 year old son, who I decided I didn't want to accompany me on the trip to prison. As I hugged him and kissed him goodbye, shame and remorse flooded by entire being. I couldn't believe how my life had taken such a terrible turn. Worst of all not only did my situation affect me, it also caused my child to suffer.

The incredible stress of being indicted and sentenced created extreme turmoil in my life. So much so that the man who I thought I'd spend the rest of my life with bailed out on me, along with others whom once held me in esteem. Regardless of how close we once were, some chose to listen to the government's embellished accusations, which the media repeatedly highlighted. A few months prior, I met a really nice guy who wasn't deterred by my mishaps. We were able to spend a quiet night together the night before my surrender, which helped me to emotionally prepare to complete this dreaded next chapter of my life.

Early on the morning of March 27, I met up with my two older sisters and their husbands. Together we took the two hour drive to Danbury. Arriving at the facility at approximately 9 a.m., I said my final tearful goodbyes and presented myself to the CO (Correctional Officer) in the lobby of the FCI. The female Correctional Officer (CO) took my drivers license and alerted the Receiving & Discharge (R&D) Officer of my arrival. Within minutes another CO from R&D came out to the lobby, handcuffed me behind my back and escorted me to the R&D area. With handcuffs wrapped around my wrists, reality quickly sunk in. I was no longer a free woman. I was now the property of the Bureau of Prisons (BOP).

Once seated in the R&D area, which is a small group of rooms that resemble a medical office, I was uncuffed and asked a series of questions about my personal history and my crime. My advocate had warned me to always be truthful to the staff and accept responsibility. He had explained that they have a copy of all my personal history, which is listed in my Pre-Sentence Investigative Report (PSR or PSI), so lying to staff would only create future problems for me. Therefore, I answered all of the questions accurately, even those that were humiliating.

After answering questions and filling out paperwork, I was told to put the few belongings I came in with on a table and asked to remove all my clothing. I nervously placed the two pair of eyeglasses I had on the table along with my small gold hoop earrings, a typed list of names and addresses of family and friends, the papers proving payment of my restitution of $59,213 and 10 days worth of prescription medication all in original bottles. I was advised by my advocate that these items would be allowed in. He also advised that I should mail myself the same papers along with some reading books, photos and magazines in case I was not allowed to bring in my contact list and documents as each intake officer can have a different idea of what is allowed. The day before I arrived at prison, I stopped off at the post office to ensure I would receive my package right away.

After leaving my personal items on the table, the much feared strip search was next. Although I imagined the worst, it didn't end up to be nearly as degrading as I had imagined. I was told to stand in front of the CO totally naked, run my fingers through my hair several times and open my mouth to allow the officer to look inside. With my arms stretched out, I had to turn my palms up and down then lift my arms over my head and lift up the soles of my feet. Last, I was asked to spread my buttocks and cough. The process lasted only a couple of minutes.

Handed a stiff, dark green two-piece uniform, socks and a pair of blue slip-on sneakers, I was officially a registered prisoner in the facility. The CO allowed me to keep my white panties and sports bra, because they had no lace or embellishments. I was given a box to ship out the clothes I came in

CHAPTER 3: STARTING THE PRISON JOURNEY

with. I was told to send them to my next of kin or I could donate them. I chose to send them to my sister. In addition, I received a form 440 which listed all the items I came in with. I was told I should keep this form at all times to prove that the items I was allowed to enter with were not contraband (unauthorized items).

Dressed in my new prison uniform, I was escorted into a room where my fingerprints and my photo were taken. After completing this process, I was issued the classic orange Bureau of Prisons I.D. card. I was then escorted into another room where I completed an interview with a member of the medical staff. She asked me several questions about my health and the prescription medication I was taking, and she administered a TB test.

My prison advocate had warned me that the medical technician would do an evaluation to see if I was suicidal or under the influence of drugs or alcohol. He strongly recommended that I report clean and sober, or I would risk losing my Camp status. He had also warned me that I should wean myself off of any medication for anxiety and a sleep aide that I was prescribed because the BOP limits the scope of medications that inmates are allowed to take.

After successfully passing the medical screening, I was introduced to my Case Manager, which is the individual who deals with the processing of papers for intake and release. I was asked to fill out more papers and I was given a PAC #. It is the number that inmates use along with their 8-digit inmate number to access the telephone and email service. I was advised to memorize it as I would use it frequently. I quietly recognized that I'd now be identified by a number, which I'd have to be able to recite if asked by staff.

The complete process of intake took several hours due to technical difficulties with fingerprinting and processing my ID card. I exited the building, given an oversized winter coat, at approximately 2 p.m. Instructed to walk up to the Camp with a bedroll in a laundry bag, I was sent out the side door.

It was a really weird feeling. After being handcuffed and processed, I was now set free and told to walk up a hill unaccompanied, to enter the Camp. I have to admit I had mixed feelings. I wanted to run away and never come back, but I knew I wouldn't be able to handle the consequences.

Feeling desperate and lonely, I walked up the hill in the freezing cold in my oversized coat dreading the rest of my journey.

When I finally approached the Camp door, I was greeted by a CO. I walked through the large visiting room where I met the head orderly, an inmate who assists the Camp Counselor with new inmates. She walked me through the Camp which appeared to be one long hallway. There were 12 rooms raised up half a level on one side of the building that housed inmates. Offices were lined up on the other side of the hallway and the downstairs consisted of three dormitory style housing areas. I was shown my room on the upper level and given a post it note with my room number and bed assignment written on it.

I was told new inmates are always housed in "Rooms" on the first level of the Camp. The rooms hold bunk beds and lockers for 6-8 inmates along with a chair for each set of bunk beds. The chair is used mostly to assist in getting up and down from the top bunk. New arrivals are housed in rooms anywhere from a few weeks to a few months. Then they are assigned to a two person cubicle in the dormitory style housing areas in the basement. I was the only inmate housed in this particular room.

I made my way to the kitchen where there were two women who my advocate had alerted to my arrival. To my surprise, these women were happy to meet me. They warmly embraced me, fed me, and provided me a bag full of items donated by other inmates to ease my transition. I was happy to receive the items because I only got a mini bag of toiletries, including a miniature toothbrush, with a tiny package of toothpaste, a tiny package with one shower worth of shampoo and a mini bar of soap. These items alone would never have lasted until I got to shop at Commissary, which occurs only once a week and would not be until Tuesday. I was grateful to receive the hygiene items, shower shoes, and gym clothing that the women had collected for me. I was happy to discover that I didn't have to sleep in the stiff dark green, prison clothing that night. These wonderful women also sent another women, who was an "expert" in making up a bed according to BOP standards, to my room to assist me with making up the top bunk I was assigned.

I got lost in time talking to my fellow inmates. Within a few hours I no longer felt like I was in prison. It felt like I was away on a retreat with old friends. The women became my angels in disguise. They helped to erase the pain I originally encountered.

After standing up to be counted at 4 p.m., nineteen women came together to throw a party for a woman who was leaving the next day. Because my room was unoccupied, besides my bunk, they decided it would be a perfect place for a party. I was amazed to see all the food and treats that the women prepared using a microwave oven and lots of creativity. I actually felt like I was at a party, which was unbelievable to me. At that moment, I knew my experience was not going to be as bad as I thought.

Although I worried I would have great difficulty sleeping, I slept like a baby my first night in prison. Day one in prison was over and I had survived. One day down and a couple hundred left to go!

REMANDED AT SENTENCING - A DIFFERENT PERSPECTIVE
By Jamila T. Davis

Unlike Lisa, I wasn't so lucky to gain the privilege of self-surrendering. When I was sentenced on July 16, 2008 at the New Jersey District Court in Newark, New Jersey, I was remanded to the U.S. Marshals, immediately handcuffed and ushered into a holding cell in the basement of the court that resembled a dungeon. I remained there for several hours until another U.S. Marshal picked a group of us up in a van and took us to the Essex County Jail where I was stripped, processed, and given a jail jump suit and a prison bed roll.

I remained at the Essex County jail for a little over three weeks housed with both state and federal inmates, until I was designated by the BOP to FCI Danbury. At that point, I was picked up, shackled (both feet and hands) and escorted by the Marshals to an airfield in New York. We drove in the U.S. Marshal's transport van, which resembles a dog cage for humans. Both men and women are transported together and driven to the air lift. The Feds have a transport system offenders call "Con Air" just as described in the famous movie. Inmates from all over the country are shackled in chains and driven to the airlift where they either meet another van or board the plane to go to their prison destinations.

The image of the uniformed officers armed with long rifles will forever remain in my mind. It was like a scene straight out of the movies. Hardened criminals with long sentences and violent records have a black box that holds their arms and prevents them from escaping. As we reached the air field and I took note of all the chained men and women, I felt like I was in a modern day scene of the show "Roots," which was based on Alex Haley's book that replicated slavery.

I was instructed to exit the van we were driven to the airlift in and was escorted onto a prison bus. At that point I was under the supervision of prison officials. The bus drove me to the doors of the Danbury Federal Prison, where I was processed and sent to the Special Housing Unit (SHU), because the prison had no available beds. I was strip searched and placed in an orange two piece suit and sent to what appeared to be a dreary hole with a bunk bed. For a little over a week, I remained in a dingy cell that encompassed a bunk bed, toilet and small sink. I was allowed out once a day at 6 a.m. for an hour to exercise in the recreation area on the roof. Confined to the SHU, my meals were all delivered to me through a slot in the cell and even bathing was limited. I was only able to take a shower three times a week while escorted to the shower area in handcuffs. This experience made me feel like a cast member on the television show "Oz".

All night in the SHU, I listened to what appeared to be lesbian lovers, who had fought and were serving disciplinary sanctions, tell each other "I love you baby" while sharing horrifying stories with each other about their experiences in prison. I was sick to my stomach imagining this would be how I would spend the rest of my lengthy sentence.

Just when I thought I could no longer bear the pain of this experience, the door of my cell popped open and I was finally released from my cage. I quickly grabbed my bed roll and headed off to the Danbury FCI compound prison where I officially started my prison journey.

PRACTICAL TIPS FOR SELF-SURRENDERING

- Do not bring your Pre-sentence Investigation Report (PSR) or Judgment and Commitment Order (J&C) with you to the prison, as it will not be allowed in the facility.
- Wear clothing that you don't mind being discarded, as all clothes are taken and shipped home or donated according to your direction.
- Arrive to the facility 9 a.m. - 11 a.m. to avoid being temporarily placed in the SHU.
- Bring a letter from your doctor(s) regarding your current medications or required medical equipment, if necessary.
- Bring cash with you so the funds will automatically be placed on your Commissary account and you can purchase your belongings.
- Bring a list of your contacts, including name, mailing address, email address and phone number.
- Before entering prison, mail yourself your contact list that includes name, mailing address, email address and phone number, medication list, up to five (5) soft cover reading books and/or up to five (5) magazines. Do not mail more than 5 books, magazines or a combination of both at a time and on the package write "Authorized BOP material." If you decide to send yourself pictures, send no more than 25 pictures at a time or the package will be rejected.
- Remove hair extensions and earrings or rings from body piercings, as they will not be allowed in.

Below you will find a list of items that you will be allowed to take into the prison with you:
- A set of dentures with a plastic case.
- Two pair of eyeglasses with cases (no tinted eyeglasses or contact lenses are permitted except for rare optical conditions.)
- A few photos of family and friends (Polaroid photos are not allowed).

- Female inmates can wear a plain, no frills, no wire white bra and white panties that do not have lace or a logo on them.
- A plain wedding band, without stones or raised surfaces, that is valued under $100.
- A plain religious medallion, without stones, that is valued under $100.
- A soft covered religious text such as a Bible or prayer book.
- Medical and/or orthopedic devices, including prescriptions. Prescription medications should be in their original labeled containers, with no more than a 10 day supply.

*Note - It is suggested that in addition to bringing in cash, ask a family member to wire money via Western Union to shop at the Commissary after you have self-surrendered. Money can be sent through Western Union's or MoneyGram Quick Collect Service utilizing the following information:

Code City: FBOP
Code State: DC
Inmate Name
Inmate Registration Number

KEY TERMS AND DEFINITIONS

COMMISSARY - The BOP store inmates shop at during designated days and times.

CONTRABAND - Items not allowed in a BOP facility including all items inmates were not authorized to bring into the facility, are not able to purchase on Commissary and modified items. Items taken out of a designated work area or from Food Service are also considered contraband.

INTAKE SCREENING - The process that is undertaken when a new inmate enters a facility, which includes being photographed, fingerprinted and strip-searched. It also includes a medical screening and psychological interview.

PAC (PHONE ACCESS CODE) AND PIN NUMBER - The numbers assigned to inmates by the BOP that allows access to telephone, email and Commissary accounts.

PRE-SENTENCE REPORT (PSR) - Also known as the Pre-Sentence Investigative Report (PSI). A report prepared by the U.S. Probation Department prior to an offender's sentencing that includes personal history and the details of the offense committed, among other important information. The PSR is heavily utilized by the Judge, BOP, U.S. Probation and prison staff.

RECEIVING AND DISCHARGE (R&D) - The area where inmates both enter a federal facility and exit upon release. It is also the designated area where intake screening takes place.

REGISTRATION NUMBER - The 8-digit identification number assigned to each inmate by the U.S. Marshal Service. It is the number that is printed on the inmate's identification which is included on all inmate documentation or correspondence, including mail.

SPECIAL HOUSING UNIT (SHU) - Also referred to as the 'hole.' An undesirable, segregated area of the prison where inmates serve time on disciplinary sanctions.

Chapter 4
Day 2

Getting Acquainted with Prison Life and Knowing What to Expect

To my surprise, I survived day one in prison and so will you! Day two was also an adventure, albeit not as scary. After the 5 a.m. count, I attended an early bird yoga class led by a lovely woman whom I met at the social gathering in my room the prior evening. Thankfully, one of the many items given to me was a pair of sneakers. I was so very grateful to receive them because I would not have had the opportunity to take advantage of the Recreation Department's exercise programs without them. In Danbury, new sneakers require a special order Cop Out which can take quite awhile, so consider yourself fortunate should you receive a good used pair. Although I self surrendered on March 27, I didn't receive my new sneakers from Commissary until June 3. Danbury, being a smaller Camp seems to have fewer Commissary options. In speaking with transferred inmates, every other Camp in the Bureau of Prisons has a better Commissary selection. (More on Commissary in Chapter 7).

The days can seem very long in the beginning without exercise and especially outdoor activity. Danbury, as most Camps in the BOP, has an outdoor track and fitness center. FCI facilities generally have some outdoor recreation opportunities but not as large and diverse as an FPC. In addition, there are various exercise classes offered at most facilities including step aerobics, interval training, yoga and Pilates. Basically, whatever skill set inmates possess and are willing to voluntarily instruct is what is offered.

I was called to laundry to "change out" just before lunch on day two. This is the process where you are issued your Government clothing. Here's what I was given:

CHAPTER 4: GETTING ACQUAINTED WITH PRISON LIFE AND KNOWING WHAT TO EXPECT

- 4 Green elastic waist pants
- 2 Short sleeved button down green shirts
- 2 Long sleeved button down green shirts
- 4 Green T-shirts
- 3 Panties
- 3 Sport bras
- 4 Pair of socks
- 1 Pair Black steel toed work shoes

Do not expect the clothing to fit you. I called the pants "clown pants" because they were ridiculously large, ill-fitting and likely made for men's bodies. It took me several months to finally acquire two pair of pants and two shirts with a satisfactory fit. I found a pair of size small pants on the garbage can between dorms after I convinced myself small pants didn't exist in the BOP. "Garbage picking" is a common practice in Federal prison. Inmates place unwanted items on top of garbage cans in the dorm areas for other inmates to peruse. If you need it, take it! Garbage picking also netted me a great winter hat, shorts and hair rollers.

After being dressed out, I went straight to work inputting my contact list on the Trust Fund Limited Inmate Computer System (TRULINCS). I brought a typed list of all my contacts with me at surrender, so it was relatively simple to input the information. There is a time limit on each session an inmate can use the computer, so I had to return several times that day before completing my list. The inmate computer network provides access to Commissary account balances, telephone, TRULINCS and a media list for MP3 players purchased on Commissary as well as holding your personal contact list. Each contact may contain the following fields: name, 2 mailing addresses, 2 email addresses, and 2 telephone numbers; however, there is a limit to the number of contacts, email addresses and telephone numbers you can store. You may input up to 100 addresses and 30 email addresses and phone numbers. All outgoing mail requires a printed label, so all contacts you plan on staying in touch with must be entered on this list.

Upon entering an email address of a contact, TRULINCS sends a system generated message to your contact directing them to the Corrlinks website www.corrlinks.com to set up an account for email contact with you. Prior to surrender, I sent out a mass email to everyone who I would eventually include on my contact list explaining the TRULINCS System as best I could and asking them to be on the look out for the system generated message. (More on communicating with the outside world in Chapter 6).

I also set up my telephone account the day before and was excited to speak to my family to let them know I was safe. On the first day, I would not have been able to call my son and my siblings without breaking down, but the next day I was determined to be strong. You need to have money on your account to use the TRULINCS and Corrlinks systems. I set up a Western Union account online days before I arrived and reviewed with my cousin when and how to deposit money. Timing is important because if the money arrives in your account before you are entered into the federal system, it will be returned to the sender. I advised my cousin to add $300 initially to my account on the afternoon of my surrender and an additional $300 the next morning. Figuring $320/monthly for Commissary needs, $69 for 300 minutes of telephone use per month and unlimited email at 5 cents per minute maximum, or 600 TRULINCS for a cost of $30.

While waiting for my contact list to be approved so I could make my first call, I occupied myself in the library. I mailed myself books and magazines before I left, but having not received them yet, I decided to pick out some books to read in the interim. The library was quiet because everyone is working between the hours of 7:30 a.m. and 3 p.m. except those who are unable to work medically, those who are considered Admission & Orientation (A&O) and those in between work shifts. (Chapter 5 of this guide will cover the A&O process in detail). A new inmate can expect an A&O group orientation and to be medically cleared within the first 28 days of arrival. Until then, it is often difficult to find ways to pass the time. I found that exercising, reading, writing and volunteering made the time go by a whole lot faster.

My first morning, I wasn't aware that breakfast was served on weekdays from 6:15 a.m. - 7:15 a.m. until it was too late, but I was determined to make main line lunch, which is served from 11:00 a.m. to 11:30 a.m. The dining hall looks like a large school cafeteria with an area for eating. Inmates line up and are able to choose their selection of food based on the national BOP menu. Short line is an early lunch period for kitchen workers to eat prior to having to serve main line.

During the period of time you are considered A&O status, you will likely familiarize yourself with the facility and the rules just as I did. When you have an actual orientation, you will be able to ask questions to staff members representing various departments, although I wouldn't suggest asking too many questions in front of other inmates so you don't appear overzealous. It's best to note who each official is and ask your question or express your concern during their office hours or when they make themselves available during main line lunch line.

You will find your name on the Call Out sheet almost daily during A&O status. A mandatory inmate appointment set by one of the BOP departments such as medical is called a Call Out. The Call Out sheet is posted electronically each afternoon on the Bulletin Board via TRULINCS for the following day appointments. Most often a printed copy is also on display outside of the CO's office. You will see your name and your inmate ID number along with a time and code of where you should report. Your first Call Outs will be medical, dental and psychology. It is extremely important you check the Call Out sheet each day because if you miss an appointment you may be given a "shot," or incident report. (Shots and incident reports are described in Chapter 5.)

I finally attended the day long A&O presentation, 23 days into my sentence, where we viewed a short video and listened to numerous staff members explain the functions of their department. After attending A&O, you are expected to know and follow the rules. Truthfully, you should already be familiar with the rules to avoid any early shots or incident reports. For example, a fellow inmate who unknowingly allowed someone to use her telephone account on the first day of her incarceration lost her computer and telephone privileges for 6 months. Consequently, she was only able to communicate with her family through handwritten letters that often took one to two weeks to reach them through snail mail.

Within days of attending the A&O presentation, you will be given a work assignment. You may submit a Cop Out for a position prior to being assigned a job. A Cop Out is officially form BP-A148 and is completed in paper or electronic format by an inmate to voice a complaint or make a request. If you have had the opportunity to talk to other inmates and know you would like to work in a particular area of the prison, complete a Cop Out for that position and submit it to the staff Foreman of that area. You may put the Cop Out in the mail box, which is usually located in close proximity to the CO's office or you may give it to that department's inmate clerk to present to the Foreman. Your best option would be to complete a "Request to Staff" electronically through email in addition to writing a paper Cop Out. There are no guarantees in prison you will be assigned to an area of your expertise or choosing. In some instances, exactly the opposite may be true depending on the supervising staff. For instance I submitted a Cop Out to the Education Department prior to being assigned a job. Despite the fact I have a Master of Science degree in Education and over 30 years of classroom teaching experience on the elementary, high school and college level, I was assigned to work in the Electric Shop. Conversely, a woman with a prison-earned GED was given a job in the Education Department. I learned early on qualifications alone don't determine job placement in the prison world. Regardless of your job assignment, make the best of it, work diligently, learn something and earn a very little bit of money in the process. The best thing about prison employment to me was that in some instances you are given the opportunity to help other inmates and that made it worth it. Since the Electric Shop is located outside of the Camp facility, a change of scenery each weekday was refreshing. A prison bus transports inmates to and from the Camp to the Shop area, which is located on the other side of the FCI compound. Because the FCI, to which the Camp is affiliated, now houses men, the Camp inmates are generally no longer allowed to walk to and from the Shop area.

SOME THINGS I LEARNED IN MY FIRST FEW DAYS OF PRISON . . . . . .

Be mindful of asking too many questions, it may make you appear to be a rat. Mind your own business and do your own time. Don't ask about anyone's charges and you will notice that very few inmates will ask about your charges. In time, others will share their information with you, but don't ask. There are a few women with whom I spent quite a bit of time with while

CHAPTER 4: GETTING ACQUAINTED WITH PRISON LIFE AND KNOWING WHAT TO EXPECT

incarcerated and I still don't know what they were charged with, nor do I want to know. The only questions that I feel are okay to ask are "How much time did you get?" and "How long have you been down?"

Do not talk about what you have in the outside world like money, cars and homes. It could potentially make others jealous and possibly make you a target for extortion.

Don't cut in line for meals, laundry or any line at all. You will get fed, you will get your laundry and you will still have plenty of time to spare. In fact, you may end up having too much time on your hands.

Don't reach across another inmate's food under any circumstances. I learned that the hard way; one day I was reaching for the hot water dispenser while another inmate was cooking at the microwave, she let me know in no uncertain terms I could have gotten hair in her food. I apologized immediately and never did it again. Fortunately, she did not hold a grudge and was always cordial and helpful to me.

Always remember you are an inmate, not the police. Therefore, if you have a problem with another inmate, try your best to settle it between yourselves. Do not go to the CO, unless the matter has gotten extremely out of hand. If you hear or see something that is against the rules, keep it to yourself or risk being ostracized. The only exception is if your life is in immediate danger, which is not likely to happen if you use common sense in all of your dealings with others. There are others who will make comments to you should they notice you are not observing a minor rule such as bringing your apple back from lunch. A gentle reminder to them that they have eight digits after their name, just as you do, should suffice.

Since there is no privacy in prison, you will likely hear conversations and witness illegal actions.

Steer clear and don't react in any way. Responding to overheard conversations or actions with facial expressions or words may put you at risk for a future confrontation.

Try not to complain too often. You are not the only person who doesn't want to be in prison and no matter how bad you think your life is, someone else has it much worse. I attended a weekly sharing program led by four amazing, caring volunteers and after listening to dreadful stories of so many women, I realized my life was not so bad and could have been worse. I quickly learned not to complain about my one year sentence or my son's failing Algebra grade. If you must complain, do it through journal writing, phone calls or email. Always be cautious when "venting" to the outside world because telephone calls and emails are monitored.

Be respectful. Most fights in prison happen because one inmate feels a lack of respect from another inmate. If your "bunkie," also known as cell mate or "celly," is asleep at count time, wake him or her up. If an inmate saves a chair in the television room, don't sit in that chair. If you're washing several bowls, cups or utensils at the sink and someone wants to rinse out just one cup, invite them to go before you.

The biggest courtesy you can extend is the courtesy flush. When using the toilet, flush often to keep odors at bay. Living next to a bathroom for more than six months, I can personally attest to the importance of that courtesy.

Generally, you should maintain a quiet confidence, stay under the radar and simply blend into the crowd as best you can. Trust no one and never let your guard down. If you keep all of these helpful hints in mind, your incarceration will definitely flow much smoother.

SPENDING TIME IN A FEDERAL CORRECTIONAL INSTITUTION (FCI)
By: Jamila T. Davis

Unlike Lisa, I spent my first year in prison in an FCI which is a low security institution. The women with whom I was housed with had way more of a "street edge" then Campers do. From the moment I was released from the SHU to the prison grounds, which is called the compound, I felt like fresh meat, as I endured the intense stares of many women.

Luckily, a few girls, who I was temporarily housed with at the County Jail took me under their wings. They immediately embraced me, fed me and gave me clothes to wear. I was extremely relieved to exit the stringent confines of the SHU, so the environment did not bother me much.

The first thing I noticed was the large amount of couples I saw. No exaggeration, it appeared that 85% of the compound was coupled up in relationships. I had to make a conscious effort not to stare, but it was extremely abnormal behavior to me back then.

CHAPTER 4: GETTING ACQUAINTED WITH PRISON LIFE AND KNOWING WHAT TO EXPECT

In the FCI, there is what are called "10 minute moves," which is controlled movement. From 7:30 a.m. until 3:00 p.m. every hour on the hour there are 10 minute moves to get to your desired location before all the doors in all the areas are locked. Therefore, you will need a wrist watch to monitor your time closely.

My first day on the compound I ran into a woman who did my hair in the free world. I went into the hair care area to make a hair appointment when she noticed me. Joyfully, she embraced me and began to tell the other women who I was. Unknown to me at the time, she also shared some personal information about me like the fact that she braided my fiancee's hair, who was a professional football player for the New York Giants. She had also talked about the lavish condo we lived in and the luxury cars we drove.

The next day, after settling in, I received intense stares from many of the women and one girl approached me accusing me of snitching on her to the Lieutenant. At the time, I had no clue who the Lieutenant was. Luckily I had an aggressive friend who stood up for me and handled the matter. She also revealed to me the jealousy that was stirred by the hair dresser who revealed my former social status.

I managed to overcome the initial strife I encountered and quickly learned prison is not a place to share former life success stories. For the most part, I survived by keeping to myself and staying out of sexual relationships with others.

Unlike the Camp, there are many more predators in an FCI. They will watch your shopping habits and scheme on ways to hustle you out of your money. My advice is to remain low key and stay out of the business of others. Refrain from making negative comments about anyone, even if you are asked. Mind your business and be respectful of those around you. Never belittle those you feel may be less fortunate than you. If you do, you may open the doors to constant chaos and turmoil.

Be sure not to jump ahead of others on lines and if you can, refrain from the TV rooms and limit your use of the microwave. Many of the fights that occur in the FCI are about TV issues and microwaves.

Lastly, try your best not to appear frightened. Speak up for yourself when necessary, but be respectful in your delivery. Even if you don't have great courage, inmates typically dislike bullies, so someone will likely come to your aide. Be kind and your kindness will keep you protected and most likely be reciprocated.

Life in an FCI may be a major culture shock for many but you can get through it. I did!

KEY TERMS AND DEFINITIONS

ADMISSIONS & ORIENTATION (A&O) - New inmate orientation process. All new inmates are placed on A&O status until they complete the A&O program, which includes a presentation introducing the prison staff and policies of the institution.

BUNKIE - An inmate's cell mate that is housed in the same immediate area. Generally, bunkies share the same bunk bed.

CALL OUT - The computerized listing of appointments for inmates that can be checked daily through TRULINCS. Also known as Change Sheet.

CHANGE OUT - The process where inmates exchange the clothes they initially receive at R&D for official standard prison uniforms, T-shirts and undergarments. Also known as Dress Out.

CHANGE SHEET - The daily computerized listing of changes that affect inmates such as job changes.

CHOW HALL - The lunch room inmates eat in, also referred to as the "Dining Hall."

COMMISSARY - The BOP store inmates shop at during designated days and times.

COMPOUND - The grounds of the prison facility.

COP OUT - The form completed by an inmate to make a request of staff. Officially called a BPA-148

CORRLINKS - The Internet company that manages all inmate public messages (email). The company's official website is www.corrlinks.com.

SNITCH - An inmate that cooperates with the Government or informs prison officials of the improper behavior of other inmates.

SPECIAL HOUSING UNIT (SHU) - Also referred to as the 'hole.' An undesirable, segregated area of the prison where inmates serve time on disciplinary sanctions.

TRULINCS - Trust Fund Limited Inmate Computer System (TRULINCS) Allows inmates to access multiple services including: Account Transactions, Bulletin Board, Contact List, Law Library, Manage Funds, Manage TRU-Units, Prescription Refill, Print, Public Messaging (email), Request to Staff and Survey.

Chapter 5
Admissions & Orientation (A&O)

Learning the Basic Rules and Regulations

The key to survival in federal prison is knowing the rules and following them. There are hefty sanctions for prisoners who are found guilty of violating BOP regulations, including losing good time credit, serving time in the SHU, being shipped to higher security level facilities and the loss of email, visits and phone privileges. Therefore, it is vital inmates understand what is required and stay incident free.

In this chapter we will explore the basic rules and regulations of the BOP, which are normally presented during A&O. As explained previously, all new inmates are required to participate in the A&O program within 28 days of their arrival to prison. A&O is generally a full day session where new inmates learn the rules and regulations of the prison and are introduced to the prison staff. During this session, inmates are shown an orientation video and introduced to the programs and services that the facility has to offer. Upon completion of the session, inmates are required to sign a document stating that they know and understand all the BOP rules. Once this statement is signed, inmates are held responsible for following prison regulations.

SANITATION

Sanitation is a key responsibility of inmates. Living in shared quarters requires each inmate to play a role in keeping the area tidy. Inmates are required to make their beds, military style, prior to 7:30 a.m. work call. Each inmate is also required to sweep and mop their cell or cubicle floor, remove trash and ensure their living areas are sanitary. Lockers must be neatly arranged inside and nothing is to be kept on top of the locker except for one

CHAPTER 5: LEARNING THE BASIC RULES AND REGULATIONS

religious book and an alarm clock. COs do constant inspections to ensure inmate living quarters are clean. It can be quite embarrassing to be publicly reprimanded for being unclean. Your bunkie, who shares the immediate area, may become angry or frustrated if you do not handle your share of the cleaning duties. Therefore, it is recommended you clean your living quarters daily. Keep your area neat and clean up after yourself where ever you go throughout the prison.

INMATE ATTIRE AND LAUNDRY

Inmates are required to wear their proper uniform during work hours, which is typically 7:30 a.m. to 3:00 p.m. Proper uniform consists of an institution issued khaki shirt and pants and work boots or shoes. Shirts are required to be tucked into your pants and you must where your I.D. around your neck on a lanyard I.D. protector, which is given to all inmates at intake. If you misplace your I.D. you must report it to your Counselor and pay a $5.00 fee for a replacement I.D. card. The funds will be withdrawn from your Commissary account. Your clothing is expected to be clean, properly fitted and presentable.

In the event your uniform becomes damaged or no longer fits, there is a weekly laundry exchange where you can trade them for newer or better fitting clothing. There are also scheduled laundry services, usually in the a.m. before work call, where you drop off your clothes three times a week to be washed. Ask a fellow inmate or CO for the posted laundry schedule and procedures to obtain current information about inmate laundry services in your facility.

INMATE COUNT

Each BOP institution is required to count inmates a minimum of five times each day. On weekends and holidays, an additional count is conducted at 10:00 a.m. It is vital you familiarize yourself with count times and count procedures as being out of your assigned area during count time will result in automatic disciplinary action with high sanctions.

All inmates are required to stand at bedside during official counts held at 4:00 p.m. and 9:00 p.m. and on weekends or holidays at 10:00 a.m., 4:00 p.m. and 9:00 p.m. During count time, all inmates must be silent and visible for the officers to count. If inmates are disruptive or out of area during count, they may be issued an incident report for obstructing the count.

CALL OUTS/CHANGE SHEETS

Call Outs are scheduled appointments (which include medical, dental, educational, team meeting, etc.) that prison staff schedule for inmates. The schedule is posted by 4 p.m. on the TRULINCS inmate Bulletin Board and on the unit bulletin boards for appointments that will occur the next day. It is the responsibility of inmates to read the Call Out sheet daily, know the time of their appointment and show up for the appointment on time. If you miss an appointment posted on the Call Out sheet, you may be issued an incident report.

Behind the Call Out is a section called the Change Sheet. The Change Sheet reflects changes in education status and changes in work assignment. It is important that in addition to checking the Call Out sheet, inmates also monitor the Change Sheet to ensure they are in the proper assigned areas when required.

CONTRABAND

Items inmates are not allowed to have in the facility are considered contraband. These include all items inmates were not authorized to bring into the facility, are not able to purchase on Commissary as well as items that are not to be taken out of a designated work area for personal use. According to BOP regulations, contraband includes materials prohibited by law or by regulation or material which can reasonably be expected to cause physical injury or adversely affect the security, safety or good order of the institution.

Food service items that are provided in the Dining Hall are not allowed in inmate living quarters. If you take any of these items out of the Dining Hall, they are considered contraband. If you get caught with them, you may receive an incident report. Additionally, work tools and materials

CHAPTER 5: LEARNING THE BASIC RULES AND REGULATIONS

used on your job site are not to be taken out of the work area. If these items are found in your living quarters, they are considered contraband and an incident report may be written.

In sum, only Government issued clothing or hygiene items purchased on Commissary, plus books, magazines, newspapers, a calendar or legal paperwork sent in are property inmates are allowed in living areas.

SHAKEDOWNS

Inmates are subject to random searches where there is reasonable belief that contraband may be concealed on their person or a good opportunity for concealment has occurred. Additionally, BOP staff or officers may search an inmate's housing and work area randomly without the inmate's presence, per BOP policy. COs are issued a master key to open lockers as needed.

Accordingly, be mindful that you are a prisoner and you have limited rights when it comes to searches. Therefore, be cautious of what items you keep in your living area and on your person. Be cooperative if you are asked to cooperate in a random search. Resisting is considered disobeying a staff member which can result in a disciplinary sanction.

DRUG SURVEILLANCE/ ALCOHOL DETECTION

Prisoners are subject to random drug tests. The central office has a system that picks inmates randomly, requiring those individuals to be tested by institution staff. In addition, staff may test an individual based on suspicion of them being under the influence. If an inmate refuses to be tested, it will result in an automatic disciplinary sanction.

OUT OF BOUNDS

Inmates who are not in their proper work area during work hours are considered out of bounds. The exceptions are if you are on a Call Out or have a medical idle or medical convalescence, which are given to inmates who have been seen by the Medical staff and have been determined to be ill.

Random census counts are conducted periodically. All areas are secured and the facility is counted. If inmates are found out of their work area, especially during a census count, it may result in a disciplinary sanction.

Additionally, inmates are not allowed to enter the housing area of other inmates who do not live in their dorm or housing unit. If you are caught in a dorm or housing unit that you do not live in, it may result in an incident report.

FIGHTING/THREATENING

Inmates are not allowed to fight, threaten or cause physical harm to another inmate. Fighting will result in an automatic disciplinary sanction.

In addition, inmates are not allowed to make bets or gamble with one another. If staff becomes aware of betting activities, it may result in a disciplinary sanction.

This concludes the basic rules inmates must follow. A vital principle to survival is showing respect to others, both staff and fellow inmates. Following this principle will keep you out of trouble. I have included the BOP Prohibited Acts and Available Sanctions Chart at the conclusion of this chapter. It is my advice you review this chart to know exactly what actions may result if you violate BOP disciplinary codes. Please note, all of the rules are not always upheld or followed by inmates. But, it's important you are aware you can be punished if a CO decides to write you up. Therefore, if you violate the BOP disciplinary codes, you are playing at your own risk. Beware!

KEY TERMS AND DEFINITIONS

ADMISSIONS & ORIENTATION (A&O) - New inmate orientation process. All new inmates are placed on A&O status until they complete the A&O program, which includes a presentation introducing the prison staff and policies of the institution.

CONTRABAND - Items not allowed in a BOP facility including all items inmates were not authorized to bring into the facility, are not able to purchase on Commissary and modified items. Items

PROHIBITED ACTS AND AVAILABLE SANCTIONS

GREATEST SEVERITY LEVEL PROHIBITED ACTS

100   Killing.

101   Assaulting any person, or an armed assault on the institution's secure perimeter (a charge for assaulting any person at this level is to be used only when serious physical injury has been attempted or accomplished).

102   Escape from escort; escape from any secure or non-secure institution, including community confinement; escape from unescorted community program or activity; escape from outside a secure institution.

103   Setting a fire (charged with this act in this category only when found to pose a threat to life or a threat of serious bodily harm or in furtherance of a prohibited act of Greatest Severity, e.g., in furtherance of a riot or escape; otherwise the charge is properly classified Code 218, or 329).

104   Possession, manufacture, or introduction of a gun, firearm, weapon, sharpened instrument, knife, dangerous chemical, explosive, ammunition, or any instrument used as a weapon.

105   Rioting.

106   Encouraging others to riot.

107   Taking hostage(s).

108   Possession, manufacture, introduction, or loss of a hazardous tool (tools most likely to be used in an escape or escape attempt or to serve as weapons capable of doing serious bodily harm to others; or those hazardous to institutional security or personal safety; e.g., hacksaw blade, body armor, maps, handmade rope, or other escape paraphernalia, portable telephone, pager, or other electronic device).

109   (Not to be used).

110   Refusing to provide a urine sample; refusing to breathe into a Breathalyzer; refusing to take part in other drug-abuse testing.

111 Introduction or making of any narcotics, marijuana, drugs, alcohol, intoxicants, or related paraphernalia, not prescribed for the individual by the medical staff.
112 Use of any narcotics, marijuana, drugs, alcohol, intoxicants, or related paraphernalia, not prescribed for the individual by the medical staff.

113 Possession of any narcotics, marijuana, drugs, alcohol, intoxicants, or related paraphernalia, not prescribed for the individual by the medical staff.

114 Sexual assault of any person, involving non-consensual touching by force or threat of force.

115 Destroying and/or disposing of any item during a search or attempt to search.

196 Use of the mail for an illegal purpose or to commit or further a Greatest category prohibited act.

197 Use of the telephone for an illegal purpose or to commit or further a Greatest category prohibited act.

198 Interfering with a staff member in the performance of duties most like another Greatest severity prohibited act. This charge is to be used only when another charge of Greatest severity is not accurate. The offending conduct must be charged as "most like" one of the listed Greatest severity prohibited acts.

199 Conduct which disrupts or interferes with the security or orderly running of the institution or the Bureau of Prisons most like another Greatest severity prohibited act. This charge is to be used only when another charge of Greatest severity is not accurate. The offending conduct must be charged as "most like" one of the listed Greatest severity prohibited acts.

AVAILABLE SANCTIONS FOR GREATEST SEVERITY LEVEL PROHIBITED ACTS

A. Recommend parole date rescission or retardation.

B. Forfeit and/or withhold earned statutory good time or non-vested good conduct time (up to 100%) and/or terminate or disallow extra good time (an extra good time or good conduct time sanction may not be suspended).
B.1. Disallow ordinarily between 50% and 75% (27-41 days) of

good conduct time credit available for year (a good conduct time sanction may not be suspended).

C. Disciplinary segregation (up to 12 months).

D. Make monetary restitution.

E. Monetary fine.

F. Loss of privileges (e.g., visiting, telephone, commissary, movies, recreation).

G. Change housing (quarters).

H. Remove from program and/or group activity.

I. Loss of job.

J. Impound inmate's personal property.

K. Confiscate contraband.

L. Restrict to quarters.

M. Extra duty.

HIGH SEVERITY LEVEL PROHIBITED ACTS

200 Escape from a work detail, non-secure institution, or other non-secure confinement, including community confinement, with subsequent voluntary return to Bureau of Prisons custody within four hours.

201 Fighting with another person.

202 (Not to be used).

203 Threatening another with bodily harm or any other offense.

204 Extortion; blackmail; protection; demanding or receiving money or anything of value in return for protection against others, to avoid bodily harm, or under threat of informing.

205 Engaging in sexual acts.

206 Making sexual proposals or threats to another.
207 Wearing a disguise or a mask.

208 Possession of any unauthorized locking device, or lock pick, or tampering with or blocking any lock device (includes keys), or destroying, altering, interfering with, improperly using, or damaging any security device, mechanism, or procedure.

209 Adulteration of any food or drink.

210 (Not to be used).

211 Possessing any officer's or staff clothing.

212 Engaging in or encouraging a group demonstration.

213 Encouraging others to refuse to work, or to participate in a work stoppage.

214 (Not to be used).

215 (Not to be used).

216 Giving or offering an official or staff member a bribe, or anything of value.

217 Giving money to, or receiving money from, any person for the purpose of introducing contraband or any other illegal or prohibited purpose.

218 Destroying, altering, or damaging government property, or the property of another person, having a value in excess of $100.00, or destroying, altering, damaging life-safety devices (e.g., fire alarm) regardless of financial value.

219 Stealing; theft (including data obtained through the unauthorized use of a communications device, or through unauthorized access to disks, tapes, or computer printouts or other automated equipment on which data is stored).

220 Demonstrating, practicing, or using martial arts, boxing (except for use of a punching bag), wrestling, or other forms of physical encounter, or military exercises or drill (except for drill authorized by staff).

221 Being in an unauthorized area with a person of the opposite sex without staff permission.

222 (Not to be used).
223 (Not to be used).

224 Assaulting any person (a charge at this level is used when less serious physical injury or contact has been attempted or accomplished by an inmate).

225 Stalking another person through repeated behavior which harasses, alarms, or annoys the person, after having been previously warned to stop such conduct.

226 Possession of stolen property.

227 Refusing to participate in a required physical test or examination unrelated to testing for drug abuse (e.g., DNA, HIV, tuberculosis).

228 Tattooing or self-mutilation.

229 Sexual assault of any person, involving non-consensual touching without force or threat of force.

296 Use of the mail for abuses other than criminal activity which circumvent mail monitoring procedures (e.g., use of the mail to commit or further a High category prohibited act, special mail abuse; writing letters in code; directing others to send, sending, or receiving a letter or mail through unauthorized means; sending mail for other inmates without authorization; sending correspondence to a specific address with directions or intent to have the correspondence sent to an unauthorized person; and using a fictitious return address in an attempt to send or receive unauthorized correspondence).

297 Use of the telephone for abuses other than illegal activity which circumvent the ability of staff to monitor frequency of telephone use, content of the call, or the number called; or to commit or further a High category prohibited act.

298 Interfering with a staff member in the performance of duties most like another High severity prohibited act. This charge is to be used only when another charge of High severity is not accurate. The offending conduct must be charged as "most like" one of the listed High severity prohibited acts.

299 Conduct which disrupts or interferes with the security or orderly running of the institution or the Bureau of Prisons

317 Failure to follow safety or sanitation regulations (including safety regulations, chemical instructions, tools, MSDS sheets, OSHA standards).

318 Using any equipment or machinery without staff authorization.

319 Using any equipment or machinery contrary to instructions or posted safety standards.

320 Failing to stand count.

321 Interfering with the taking of count.

322 (Not to be used).

323 (Not to be used).

324 Gambling.

325 Preparing or conducting a gambling pool.

326 Possession of gambling paraphernalia.

327 Unauthorized contacts with the public.

328 Giving money or anything of value to, or accepting money or anything of value from, another inmate or any other person without staff authorization.

329 Destroying, altering, or damaging government property, or the property of another person, having a value of $100.00 or less.

330 Being unsanitary or untidy; failing to keep one's person or quarters in accordance with posted standards.

331 Possession, manufacture, introduction, or loss of a non-hazardous tool, equipment, supplies, or other non-hazardous contraband (tools not likely to be used in an escape or escape attempt, or to serve as a weapon capable of doing serious bodily harm to others, or not hazardous to institutional security or personal safety) (other non-hazardous contraband includes such items as food, cosmetics, cleaning supplies, smoking apparatus and tobacco in any form where prohibited, and unauthorized nutritional/dietary supplements).

332 Smoking where prohibited.

333 Fraudulent or deceptive completion of a skills test (e.g., cheating on a GED, or other educational or vocational skills test).

334 Conducting a business; conducting or directing an investment transaction without staff authorization.

335 Communicating gang affiliation; participating in gang related activities; possession of paraphernalia indicating gang affiliation.

336 Circulating a petition.

396 Use of the mail for abuses other than criminal activity which do not circumvent mail monitoring; or use of the mail to commit or further a Moderate category prohibited act.

397 Use of the telephone for abuses other than illegal activity which do not circumvent the ability of staff to monitor frequency of telephone use, content of the call, or the number called; or to commit or further a Moderate category prohibited act.

398 Interfering with a staff member in the performance of duties most like another Moderate severity prohibited act. This charge is to be used only when another charge of Moderate severity is not accurate. The offending conduct must be charged as "most like" one of the listed Moderate severity prohibited acts.

399 Conduct which disrupts or interferes with the security or orderly running of the institution or the Bureau of Prisons most like another Moderate severity prohibited act. This charge is to be used only when another charge of Moderate severity is not accurate. The offending conduct must be charged as "most like" one of the listed Moderate severity prohibited acts.

AVAILABLE SANCTIONS FOR MODERATE SEVERITY LEVEL PROHIBITED ACTS

A. Recommend parole date rescission or retardation.

most like another High severity prohibited act. This charge is to be used only when another charge of High severity is not accurate. The offending conduct must be charged as "most like" one of the listed High severity prohibited acts.

AVAILABLE SANCTIONS FOR HIGH SEVERITY LEVEL PROHIBITED ACTS

A. Recommend parole date rescission or retardation.

B. Forfeit and/or withhold earned statutory good time or non-vested good conduct time up to 50% or up to 60 days, whichever is less, and/or terminate or disallow extra good time (an extra good time or good conduct time sanction may not be suspended).

B.1 Disallow ordinarily between 25% and 50% (14-27 days) of good conduct time credit available for year (a good conduct time sanction may not be suspended).

C. Disciplinary segregation (up to 6 months).

D. Make monetary restitution.

E. Monetary fine.

F. Loss of privileges (*e.g.*, visiting, telephone, commissary, movies, recreation).

G. Change housing (quarters).

H. Remove from program and/or group activity.

I. Loss of job.

J. Impound inmate's personal property.

K. Confiscate contraband.

L. Restrict to quarters.

M. Extra duty.

MODERATE SEVERITY LEVEL PROHIBITED ACTS

300 Indecent Exposure.

301 (Not to be used).

302 Misuse of authorized medication.

303 Possession of money or currency, unless specifically authorized, or in excess of the amount authorized.

304 Loaning of property or anything of value for profit or increased return.

305 Possession of anything not authorized for retention or receipt by the inmate, and not issued to him through regular channels.

306 Refusing to work or to accept a program assignment.

307 Refusing to obey an order of any staff member (may be categorized and charged in terms of greater severity, according to the nature of the order being disobeyed, e.g. failure to obey an order which furthers a riot would be charged as 105, Rioting; refusing to obey an order which furthers a fight would be charged as 201, Fighting; refusing to provide a urine sample when ordered as part of a drug-abuse test would be charged as 110).

308 Violating a condition of a furlough.

309 Violating a condition of a community program.

310 Unexcused absence from work or any program assignment.

311 Failing to perform work as instructed by the supervisor.

312 Insolence towards a staff member.

313 Lying or providing a false statement to a staff member.

314 Counterfeiting, forging, or unauthorized reproduction of any document, article of identification, money, security, or official paper (may be categorized in terms of greater severity according to the nature of the item being reproduced, e.g., counterfeiting release papers to effect escape, Code 102).

315 Participating in an unauthorized meeting or gathering.

316 Being in an unauthorized area without staff authorization.

B. Forfeit and/or withhold earned statutory good time or non-vested good conduct time up to 25% or up to 30 days, whichever is less, and/or terminate or disallow extra good time (an extra good time or good conduct time sanction may not be suspended).

B.1 Disallow ordinarily up to 25% (1-14 days) of good conduct time credit available for year (a good conduct time sanction may not be suspended).

C. Disciplinary segregation (up to 3 months).

D. Make monetary restitution.

E. Monetary fine.

F. Loss of privileges (e.g., visiting, telephone, commissary, movies, recreation).

G. Change housing (quarters).

H. Remove from program and/or group activity.

I. Loss of job.

J. Impound inmate's personal property.

K. Confiscate contraband.

L. Restrict to quarters.

M. Extra duty.

LOW SEVERITY LEVEL PROHIBITED ACTS

400 (Not to be used).

401 (Not to be used).

402 Malingering, feigning illness.

403 (Not to be used).

404 Using abusive or obscene language.

405 (Not to be used).

406 (Not to be used).

407 Conduct with a visitor in violation of Bureau regulations.

408 (Not to be used).

409 Unauthorized physical contact (e.g., kissing, embracing).

498 Interfering with a staff member in the performance of duties most like another Low severity prohibited act. This charge is to be used only when another charge of Low severity is not accurate. The offending conduct must be charged as "most like" one of the listed Low severity prohibited acts.

499 Conduct which disrupts or interferes with the security or orderly running of the institution or the Bureau of Prisons most like another Low severity prohibited act. This charge is to be used only when another charge of Low severity is not accurate. The offending conduct must be charged as "most like" one of the listed Low severity prohibited acts.

AVAILABLE SANCTIONS FOR LOW SEVERITY LEVEL PROHIBITED ACTS

B.1 Disallow ordinarily up to 12.5% (1-7 days) of good conduct time credit available for year (to be used only where inmate found to have committed a second violation of the same prohibited act within 6 months); Disallow ordinarily up to 25% (1-14 days) of good conduct time credit available for year (to be used only where inmate found to have committed a third violation of the same prohibited act within 6 months) (a good conduct time sanction may not be suspended).

C. Make monetary restitution.

D. Monetary fine.

E. Loss of privileges (e.g., visiting, telephone, commissary, movies, recreation).

F. Change housing (quarters).

G. Remove from program and/or group activity.

H. Loss of job.

I. Impound inmate's personal property.

J. Confiscate contraband

K. Restrict to quarters.

L. Extra duty.

Table 2. ADDITIONAL AVAILABLE SANCTIONS FOR REPEATED PROHIBITED ACTS WITHIN THE SAME SEVERITY LEVEL

Prohibited Act Severity Level	Time period For prior Offense- same code	Frequency of Repeated offense	Additional Available Sanctions
Low Severity (400 level)	6 months	2nd Offense Or 3rd Offense	1. Disciplinary segregation (up to 1 month). 2. Forfeit earned SGT or non-vested GCT up to 10% or up to 15 days, whichever is less, and/or terminate or disallow extra good time (EGT) (an EGT sanction may not be suspended). Any available Moderate severity level sanction (300 series).
Moderate severity (300 level)	12 months	2nd Offense or 3rd Offense	1. Disciplinary segregation (up to 6 months). 2. Forfeit earned SGT or non-vested GCT up to 37 1/2% or up to 45 days, whichever is less, and/or terminate or disallow EGT (an EGT sanction may not be suspended). Any available High severity level sanction (200 series).
High Severity (200 level)	18 months	2nd Offense Or 3rd Offense	1. Disciplinary segregation (up to 12 months). 2. Forfeit earned SGT or non-vested GCT up to 75% or up to 90 days, whichever is less, and/or terminate or disallow EGT (an EGT sanction may not be suspended). Any available Greatest severity level sanction (100 series).
Greatest Severity (100 level)	24 months	2nd or more Offense	Disciplinary Segregation (up to 18 months).

taken out of a designated work area or from Food Service are also considered contraband.

COUNT - The process of physically counting inmates in their housing area, which occurs at least 5 times daily. Stand up counts require the inmate to silently stand in their cell/cube while being counted.

INCIDENT REPORT - Also referred to as a "shot." A formal report written against an inmate who violates BOP rules.

OUT OF BOUNDS - A BOP infraction for inmates who are not in their properly designated area at a particular time.

RECALL - The process of inmates being called to their housing units at a particular time, usually in preparation for count.

SHAKEDOWN - When BOP staff or officers search a particular area.

SHOT - An inmate term for incident report.

SPECIAL HOUSING UNIT (SHU) - Also referred to as the 'hole.' An undesirable, segregated area of the prison where inmates serve time on disciplinary sanctions.

Chapter 6
Mail, Telephone, Email
Staying Connected with the Outside World

During your time in prison you will desire to sustain your ties with the outside world. Photos, phone calls, visits and emails will keep you connected to your loved ones and help you to escape from your mundane prison life.

In this chapter, we will explore the BOP's policies and procedures for prison mail, telephone, email and visiting. It is essential you know and follow the rules governing these areas to maintain contact with the outside world.

MAIL/OUTGOING CORRESPONDENCE

Inmates are permitted to correspond with the public, family members and others without prior approval. Inmates housed in medium or low security facilities are able to seal their mail prior to placing it in the inmate outgoing mailbox. Inmates housed in medium or high security prisons must keep their mail unsealed for staff inspection.

On the outside top left hand corner of the envelope, inmates must write out their name, inmate number, the complete name of the facility in which they are housed, along with the institution address. The name of the facility may not be abbreviated, if so, the mail will not be sent out. Additionally, all outgoing mail must have a mailing label printed out from the TRULINCS system. Without a printed label, the mail will be returned to the inmate.

Inmate correspondence must not contain threats, extortion, etc., which may result in prosecution for violation of Federal laws.

Mail service is ordinarily provided five days a week, Monday through Friday, except for holidays. A mail box is located in each facility. Generally outgoing mail must be placed in the inmate mailbox by 11:00 p.m. in order to go out the next morning.

CERTIFIED/REGISTERED MAIL

Inmates may send out certified, registered, or insured mail. These letters or packages must be sent out through the mail room during mail room open house. Refer to your institution for days and times for mail room open house.

INCOMING CORRESPONDENCE

Incoming mail is distributed Monday through Friday (except for holidays). Generally the evening watch officer distributes mail in each living unit, yet the day watch officer may voluntarily give out mail on occasion. All incoming mail must contain the inmate's name and register number to guarantee delivery.

INCOMING PUBLICATIONS

The BOP allows inmates to receive magazines, newsletters, newspapers, books and pamphlets without prior approval. These items may come directly from the publisher or from family members and friends, for those housed in a minimum or low security facility.

Inmates housed in a medium, high or administrative institution may only receive publications directly from a publisher, book store or book club.

Inmates are allowed to receive up to five (5) books or other publications in a package at a time. On the package it MUST state "Authorized BOP Material." If the package does not contain those three very important words, it may be sent back. Therefore, it is vital for your loved ones to mark your package on the front of the envelope, and make it visible for BOP staff to see it.

All inmates may receive books from publishers. Hard cover books will only be accepted directly from the publisher, book store or book club for all security levels.

OUTGOING SPECIAL MAIL

Mail sent to the U.S. Courts, Government or State officials, legislators, U.S. Congress members, Probation officers, law enforcement offices, attorneys and representatives of the news media are considered special mail. Inmates have a choice to send Special Mail through the regular inmate mail system or it can be logged by a prison official as Special Mail.

Special Mail has the benefit of not being read by prison staff and it is tracked so that there is a log of when it was sent out on your behalf. Additionally, mail to the U.S. Courts logged out as Special Mail receives the benefit of the Mailbox Rule, meaning, once the prison official receives it and logs it in as Special Mail, it is considered filed with the courts.

Each institution has its own rules for Special Mail procedures. Ask your Counselor or mail room staff for the Special Mail rules of your facility.

INCOMING SPECIAL MAIL

Inmate mail from the U.S. Courts (including Probation, an attorney and Government officials, including Congress members and the President of the United States) is given the benefit of Special Mail. But the correspondence must be marked "Special Mail - Open only in the presence of the inmate."

If the mail is properly marked, a staff member will open the mail in the inmate's presence, examining it only for contraband and then hand it over to the inmate. Special Mail can not be read by the staff, which is the benefit of the Special Mail privilege.

INMATE-TO-INMATE CORRESPONDENCE

Inmates may not write each other directly without prior approval from the institutions where they are both housed. Inmate correspondence is generally approved through the Counselor. Only immediate family members (mother, father, sibling, child or spouse) or a party in a current legal action (or witness) in which both parties are involved will be approved for inmate-to-inmate correspondence. Once approval is gained, inmates following BOP policy can correspond with one another through mail and/or email.

INMATE TELEPHONE SYSTEM - TRUFONE

Inmates are allotted 300 minutes of phone time each month, which can be used between the hours of 6:00 a.m. - 11:30 p.m. Up to 30 contacts can be placed on an inmate's telephone contact list. All calls through the inmate telephone system, TRUFONE, are subject to monitoring and recording. Inmates must contact their Counselor or Case Manager to arrange an unmonitored attorney call.

Calls are limited to fifteen (15) minutes in duration. After 15 minutes, the call will automatically be terminated. Once an inmate uses the phone, he or she will have to wait an additional 30 minutes to make another call.

Telephones are located in each housing unit. Funds for calls can be transferred out of your Commissary account or you can call collect. You are not allowed to make any three-way calls. Meaning, your loved ones can not put someone else in another location on the phone with you. Additionally, your loved ones can not call someone on another line and relay a message for you. Both of these examples are considered a three-way call which can result in disciplinary action against you.

CALL COSTS

As of December 2011, below you will find the cost for calls deducted from the Inmate Telephone System (ITS) account:
- Local - $0.06 a minute
- Long Distance - $0.23 a minute
- Canada - $0.35 a minute
- Mexico - $0.55 a minute
- International - $0.99 a minute

Collect calls range in fees from $0.06 to $0.38 a minute for local calls, depending on the state where the prison is located. Long distance collect calls are $0.56 a minute.

WAYS TO SAVE ON CALLS

A number of Internet based companies now allow you to purchase a phone number in an area code other than your own, which is linked to your current phone. This service is referred to as VoIP (Voice over Internet Protocol). Through a VoIP service, your relatives can get a local number that rings for their current land or cell phone. The number would reduce your calls from $0.23 per minute to $0.06 per minute if you are calling a U.S. number outside the local area. This reduced charge results in over a 70% savings!

Currently there is no policy in place in the BOP disallowing the use of VoIP numbers.

SETTING UP YOUR PHONE SERVICE

Once you are given your PAC number it may take up to 24 hours to access the TRULINCS System. When you are able to enter the system, you can add your contact names, addresses, telephone numbers and email addresses. After entering a contact, it may take up to 15 minutes to be accepted and approved in the system.

Once approved you are able to go to the telephone to set up phone service on the TRUFONE system. When you set up your phone service, you will be required to state your first and last name. Press 111 on the phone and wait for the prompt to enter your PAC number. Then wait for the prompt to record your name. The service will require you to repeat your name several times until your voice is identified. Once your voice is accepted, you will be able to make a phone call.

MAKING A PHONE CALL

To make a pre-paid phone call, dial your desired phone number, beginning with area code. You will be prompted to enter your PAC number.

Once you enter your PAC number you will be asked to state your name. Once your name is accepted by the system, your call will be placed. When your party answers, he or she will be required to press the number 5 to accept your call. Or, they have the option to press the number 7 to block your call. If your party blocks your call, it is difficult to have the line unblocked. Unblocking the line requires a written statement along with the telephone bill and state I.D. of the party to unblock the account.

Once your party presses the number 5, you are able to talk for up to 15 minutes.

To make a collect call, dial the number 0 and the phone number, starting with the area code, follow with the same steps as making a prepaid call.

TRANSFERRING MONEY FROM YOUR COMMISSARY ACCOUNT TO YOUR PHONE ACCOUNT

To transfer money from your Commissary account to your TRUFONE account, press the number 118. Listen for the prompt instructing you to enter your PAC number. After your PAC number is entered you will be given several recorded options. Press the number 3 to transfer funds. Wait for the prompt and enter the amount you wish to transfer in whole dollar numbers, no cents. Once you enter the desired transfer amount, the system will repeat the amount back to you along with your updated Commissary balance. If you approve the transfer, press the number 1 and listen for your updated phone balance. Transferring money for the phone can only be done through the TRUFONE system.

FINDING OUT THE AMOUNT OF MINUTES YOU HAVE

To find out the amount of minutes you have remaining press 118 and enter your PAC number. Listen for the phone prompts and press the number 5. Then you will hear a recording of the number of minutes that you have left until your revalidation date. Your revalidation date is very important. It is the day of the month that you receive a fresh batch of 300 minutes. To locate your revalidation date, log onto the inmate TRULINCS service and click the link for Account Transactions. On the top left corner of the screen, you will see a box that says revalidation date. Next to the box it will have your revalidation date. Your date is determined by multiplying the fifth number of your registration number by 3 and adding 1. e.g. If the fifth number is 6, multiply 6 x 3 and add 1, which equals 19. This means the inmate will revalidate on the 19th of each month.

TRULINCS/EMAIL

The Trust Fund Limited Inmate Computer System (TRULINCS) provides inmates with access to multiple services including: Account Transactions, Bulletin Board, Contact List, Law Library, Manage Funds, Manage TRU-Units, Music, Prescription Refill, Print, Public Messaging (email), Request to Staff and Surveys

TRULINCS computer work stations are generally in the auditorium and the recreation leisure area of the institution. To access your TRULINCS account, you will need your Phone Access Code (PAC) number, your Commissary Personal Identification Number (PIN) and Inmate Registration number. Most institutions now require your thumb finger print in replacement of your PIN number. When you enter these numbers, the system will require that you consent to the terms and conditions of TRULINCS. Once you agree, it will log you on to the system.

Once you enter the TRULINCS system, if you have new messages, the top of the screen will be highlighted in blue and display one or more options:
- You have (number) unread public message(s) in the past 31 days.
- You have (number) staff messages.
- You have new/approved/rejected contacts in this session.

These highlighted options alert you to what field you should access.

ACCOUNT TRANSACTIONS

On the Home page there is a link that reads "Account Transactions." It will allow you to search and view your Commissary account balance,

Available balance, Funds consumed for FRP payments, Pre-release Balance, Spending limit remaining balance and revalidation date.

On the top of the screen you will see a tab that reads "Telephone Account Statement." If you click on that link you will be able to access your telephone account balance and see your telephone log.

There is also a tab that reads "TRULINCS" on the top of the screen. If you click this link you can access your log of TRULINCS transactions.

Additionally, there is a link on the top of the screen that reads "Media." If you click on this link you will access a log of all your media purchases.

BULLETIN BOARD

On the home page there is a link that reads "Bulletin Board." If you click on this link you can access the inmate bulletin board which includes "News and Events" for the institution and Call Out/Change Sheets, which are posted daily.

CONTACT LIST

On the home page there is a link that reads "Contact List." If you click on this link, you can access your contact list and add new contacts.

To add new contacts, click on the "Add New Contacts" tab on the top of the screen. Then enter all your contact information and press save. Once you enter an email address, your contact will automatically be emailed a notification to accept your request through Corrlinks. (For more information go to www.corrlinks.com). Please note, you can not email anyone until the person accepts your request.

To view your contacts, click the tab that reads "All" under List Type. To view the status of an email request, click the tab that reads "Message List." To view your phone list, click the tab that reads "Phone List" under List Type.

To print a postal mailing label (which is required for all outgoing mail), after you have entered your contact, click the tab that reads "Mailing Label" under List Type then click on the name of the contact you wish to create a label for and enter the number of labels you wish to print under the "Enter Print Qty" section. Please note, you can only print 5 labels a day through the system. Once you have entered the label quantity, click the tab that reads "Print Labels." The computer will notify you that you will only be able to print labels once in this session. It will ask you to click "yes" or "no" if you want to continue, click "yes" and your labels will be processed. You can then log out and go to the printer computer. Log on to the printer computer using your PAC#, Reg# and Pin#, thumb fingerprint recognition device and click the tab that reads "Print." Then click on the label you wish to print and click on the Print tab on the top left hand side of the screen. This function will cause your labels to be printed automatically to the label machine.

LAW LIBRARY

The law library legal research service can be accessed through designated computers, usually in a separate section of the institution. (More on legal research via TRULINCS in Chapter 11).

MANAGE FUNDS

On the Home page there is a link that reads "Manage Funds." If you click on this link you will access a form BP-199 to have funds sent from your Commissary account to whomever you choose. Once you fill out the BP-199 form you will have to print it out using the printer computer. This form must be signed and given to your Counselor to process. Checks sent out of your account appear to the recipient as a U.S. Treasury check. Please note, it takes 2-6 weeks for your recipient to receive your check utilizing this method.

Through the Manage Funds section, you can also click on the link "Pre-Release Account." This link will allow you to transfer money to your Pre-Release Account, which is a voluntary savings account for inmates.

Additionally, there is an option under the Manage Funds section to access Money Gram. Federal inmates can send up to $100.00 a day through Money Gram to any individual on their email list. Each transaction costs $4.95 payable by the inmate. Utilizing this option, the funds are sent and your recipient receives email notification that the funds are available. Once the recipient checks the acceptance box in the email to accept the funds, the money can be picked up at any Money Gram location within the state in which the recipient lives.

MANAGE TRU-UNITS

On the Home page there is a link that reads "Manage TRU-Units." When you access this link, you will be able to transfer funds from your Commissary account to TRULINCS. TRU-Units can be purchased in increments of 40 for $2.00, 100 for $5.00, 200 for $10.00, 300 for $15.00 and 600 for $30.00. Each Tru-Unit will allow you one minute of access on email and 3 units will allow you to print one page on the printer.

MUSIC

Inmates are allowed to purchase music via the TRULINCS system. In order to access this option, inmates must have purchased an MP3 player from Commissary, which they have to connect to the computer station utilizing a USB cord provided. Once the MP3 player is plugged into the computer, wait for the player to read "Connected." When connected, press the link that reads "Music." It will open the Music Library.

All genres of music are available on the BOP music service. Songs cost on average between 16-30 TRU-Units, which equates to approximately $0.75 to $1.50 per song. The system gives you the option to search by Song Title, Artist and Genre. It also has a section where you can view most popular releases and new releases in a particular genre. Up to 25 songs can be stored on your Wish List to be purchased in the future. Inmates may purchase up to 15 songs per day.

In order to complete your music purchase, you need to place your desired selection into your shopping cart. Then you will be asked to enter your PAC# to complete the purchase. Once your purchase is made, the downloaded music will be transferred onto your MP3 player. Please note, often times the music you buy will not be immediately available. In that case, you will receive a message to return for your music the next day. When you come back the next day and hook up your MP3 player, your music will automatically be uploaded once you access the Music section.

Please note, your MP3 will have to be revalidated every 14 days or it will automatically shut off. To revalidate your MP3 player simply log on to the Music section and press the revalidate button on top. In a matter of seconds, your MP3 player will be revalidated.

PRESCRIPTION REFILL

On the Home page there is a link that reads "Prescription Refill." This option allows inmates to request prescription refills via TRULINCS for self-carry medications that are ready for refill through the prison pharmacy. Once the order form has been filled out and sent via TRULINCS, the pharmacy staff will process the request and inmates will be able to follow the established local procedures for picking up requested prescriptions.

PUBLIC MESSAGING/EMAIL

On the Home page there is a link that reads "Public Messaging." When inmates access this link they are automatically charged for the time they use logged on to this area.

To send an email, your contact must have accepted the email request that was automatically sent out by Corrlinks when you added the contact information into the system. Email costs one TRU-Unit per minute.

To send an email, press the link that reads "Compose." This option will allow you to choose a recipient. Then you are able to type in your message and send.

To save a message in draft, simply press the link "Save" and the message will automatically be saved in the Draft section of Public Messaging.

To print an email it must already be sent or saved in drafts. To print an email that is sent, click on "Sent Messages" then click on the email you want to print. When the email is highlighted press the "Print" link on top. A prompt will appear to confirm your desire to print. Click yes, your document will be sent to the print station.

To print an email saved in draft, click on the "Drafts" link. Then click on the desired email. Once highlighted on the print link on top, you will be asked if you are sure you want to print. If you click "yes," your desired document will be sent to the printer. Once you log out, you will be able to go to the print computer to print out this document. Please note, each page will cost you 3 TRU-Units.

REQUEST TO STAFF

On the Home page there is a link that reads "Request to Staff." This service allows inmates to correspond with staff electronically. The list of available departments varies by institution. Additionally, inmates are able to report sexual abuse and harassment directly to the Office of Inspector General (OIG). Requests to staff are limited to one request per day.

SURVEY

On the Home page there is a link that reads "Survey." This service allows inmates to take Bureau surveys. Different surveys are available periodically on the system. (re: Food service staff performance questionnaires).

VISITING

All visitors of Federal inmates are required to be approved before they can visit an inmate. To obtain approval, visitors must complete a Visiting List form that must be sent directly to the Correctional Counselor. Inmates may obtain this form from their Counselor or visitors can download and print this form online at www. bop.gov.

Background checks are run on all visiting applicants prior to approval. Once the visitor is approved, the inmate will be notified and has the obligation of notifying the visitor.

Immediate family members, which includes father, mother, stepparents, sisters, brothers, spouse, children and grandparents who raised the inmate can generally be approved without filling out a visiting form. As long as these individuals are listed on the inmate's Pre-Sentence Report (PSR) the inmate is able to fill out an immediate family visiting form and gain prompt approval.

An inmate's visiting list may include up to ten (10) other family members and friends outside of immediate family. Once approved, visitors are able to visit inmates on approved visiting days of the institution. Each institution has it's own visiting days and policies. Check your institution to gain more details.

Federal prisons generally have contact visits except for high security inmates. Kissing, embracing and hand-shaking/holding are generally allowed only upon arrival and departure. Both inmates and their visitors are required to be properly dressed. Inmates must be dressed in their complete uniform. Visitors are not allowed to wear any provocative clothing which include see through clothes, short shorts (must be halfway down the thigh), tight stretch pants or shorts (no spandex type), halter or tube tops, midrift clothing exposing the abdomen area and no strapless or open toe shoes. Additionally, visitors can not wear tan khaki clothing or white or grey sweat suits. This is to ensure that they are not mistaken for inmates.

Generally visits are limited to 3 adults, which are individuals that are sixteen years of age or older. Special permission for more than 3 adult visitors may be granted by the Unit Counselor by completing a Cop Out in advance of the visit. All adults must have proper identification which includes a valid state I.D., a valid driver's license, Government I.D. or a U.S. passport. Visitors are not allowed to bring any articles into the visiting room except for money, diapers and a baby bottle. All visitors are subject to searches and have to pass through a metal detector (for higher security facilities). Visitors are able to stay on the visit during the complete hours of visiting unless the visiting room gets full. Once full, the visitors who have been there the longest and who live the closest will be asked to leave first until enough space is gained for arriving visitors. For more information, please check your institution's visiting policies.

ATTORNEY VISITS/SPECIAL VISITS

Attorneys can request an attorney visit with inmates through the Counselor. Generally, attorney visits take place in the visiting room during regular hours. Inmates must arrange to gain permission to take legal documents to and from the visiting room with the unit team.

Special visits may be granted based upon extenuating family circumstances. This request should be made to the unit team explaining the details in order to gain approval.

KEY TERMS AND DEFINITIONS

CORRLINKS - The Internet company that manages all inmate public messages (email). The company's official website is www.corrlinks.com.

INMATE FINANCIAL RESPONSIBILITY PROGRAM - (See also Financial Responsibility Program - FRP) A systematic inmate payment program for court-ordered restitution, fines, fees and costs.

INMATE TELEPHONE SYSTEM (ITS) - The account used by inmates for telephone use within the BOP.

MAILBOX RULE - The Federal Court rule that deems legal mail filed by an inmate when it is handed to and logged in by a prison staff member.

PRE-RELEASE ACCOUNT - An account inmates may set up through TRULINCS where money can be transferred and saved for release.

SPECIAL MAIL - Mail from the U.S. Courts (Including U.S. Probation, an attorney and Government official, including Congressional members and the President of the United States) which may not be read by BOP staff. Special mail must be opened in the presence of the inmate recipient.

TRUFONE - The phone service for inmates in BOP custody, which can be utilized for inmate personal use.

Chapter 7
Commissary And Prison Meals

Buying What You Need And Eating To Survive In Prison

Contrary to popular belief, it takes money to survive in prison. Although the BOP provides free room and board along with basic clothing, there are many other essentials inmates are NOT provided. These other essentials may be purchased through Commissary.

Each Federal prison has it's own Commissary that sells a variety of items to inmates. Some of the available items include: under garments, hats, scarves, gloves, fleece jackets, towels, t-shirts, sweat pants, boots, sneakers, radios/MP3 players, greeting and playing cards, hygiene, dental, hair care, skin care products, book/stationary, grooming aids, gym bags, make-up, watches, hobby crafts, eyewear, combination locks, over the counter medications, batteries, fans, book lights, alarm clocks, chips, rice/tortillas, pasta/pizza, snacks, health foods, kosher/halal meals, produce, crackers, dairy, fish, condiments, candy, cookies, soups, meats, nuts, drinks, sweeteners, mixes/teas, coffee/cocoa, soda, ice cream, religious items, hair dye and yarn. (See sample Commissary list at the end of the chapter).

All Federal inmates are allowed to spend up to $320.00/month for Commissary. This limit is restricted to $80.00/weekly or $160.00/bi-weekly in many institutions. Funds to purchase Commissary items come out of the inmate's deposit account. The BOP maintains the inmates' monies (Deposit Fund) while incarcerated. An inmate may use funds in their account not only to purchase items from the Commissary, but also for their phone account, to purchase TRU-Units for their TRULINCS account, to purchase music, or to send funds out of the institution using a BP-199.

Commissary hours and schedules differ at each institution. Some institutions allow inmates to shop only once per week; others allow inmates to shop multiple times during the week. Re-validation schedules are posted on the TRULINCS electronic Bulletin Board at each institution. This is one of the first things new inmates should check and ask about!

In some facilities there is an assigned day and time each week when your Commissary order sheet must be turned in. Do not miss this deadline! If you do, you may not be allowed to shop. Check your institution's Commissary rules to be sure you are informed.

ESSENTIAL COMMISSARY ITEMS FOR NEW INMATES

When you first arrive at prison, expect to spend at least $320.00 to get the main items you need. Below you will find a list of common items new inmates may need:

- Hat $6.50
- Scarf $7.95
- Fleece Jacket $22.50
- Sweat Pants (2) $39.00
- Sweat Shirts (2) $33.60
- Shorts (2) $18.20
- Black Boots $69.50
- Sneakers $59.00
- Shower Shoes $1.05
- Toothpaste $2.60
- Toothbrush $0.95
- Soap (3 pk) $1.80
- Deodorant $1.80
- Shampoo $1.95
- Conditioner $1.95
- Towel $11.65
- Washcloth $1.95
- Body Lotion $2.90
- Box of Envelopes $1.80

- Writing Pad $1.05
- Watch $20.00
- Combination Lock $5.95
- Alarm Clock $10.50
- Mug $2.25
- Plastic Bowl $3.95
- Flatware (4 piece) $1.30

Total: $331.65

WAYS TO RECEIVE MONEY IN YOUR ACCOUNT

There are three ways loved ones can deposit funds into your Commissary account:

1. Checks or Money orders may be sent to the "Lock Box":
   Federal Bureau of Prisons
   Insert Valid Committed Inmate Name
   Insert Inmate 8-Digit Register Number
   Post Office Box 47401
   Des Moines, Iowa 50947-0001
   Checks and money orders should be made out to the inmate recipient's name with complete 8-digit register number. Be sure to have the sender utilize a postal money order if you want to have immediate access to the funds. All other checks or money orders will be placed on a 15-day hold. Also note, the BOP does not accept personal checks.
   Be sure the sender fills out the money order completely, including your complete name and register number. No additional items are to be placed in the envelope, as the process center in Iowa only processes money for inmates.

2. Western Union Quick Collect
   Inmates' families and friends may also send inmate's funds through Western Union's Quick Collect Program. Money sent

CHAPTER 7: BUYING WHAT YOU NEED AND EATING TO SURVIVE IN PRISON

through Western Union will automatically post on the inmate's account and will be available as cash, as long as it is sent between 7:00 a.m. and 9:00 p.m. EST seven days per week, including holidays. Funds received after 9:00 p.m. EST will be posted by 7:00 a.m. EST the following morning.
- To find the nearest Western Union location, your loved ones may call 1-800-325-6000 or go to westernunion.com.
- To complete a Western Union transaction by phone through credit/debit card, your loved ones may call 800-634-3422 and press option 2.
- To complete a Western Union transaction online, your loved ones may go to www.westernunion.com and select "Quick Collect."

For each Western Union Quick Collect transaction, the following information must be provided:
a. Valid Inmate 8-digit Register Number (enter with no spaces or dashes followed immediately by Inmate's Last Name)
b. Inmate Full Name entered on Attention line
c. Code City: FBOP
d. Code State: DC

3. Money Gram Express Payment Program
Money Gram also offers a payment program for inmates to receive money. This service works identical to Western Union. Money posted through Money Gram is also immediately available as cash if posted between 7:00 a.m. - 9:00 p.m. Transactions posted after 9:00 p.m. will post the next morning by 7:00 a.m.
   a. To find the nearest Money Gram location, your loved ones may call, 800-926-9400 or go to www.moneygram.com. A Money Gram Express Blue Form must be completed.
   b. To complete a Money Gram transaction online, your loved ones may go to www.moneygram.com/paybills.

Enter Receive Code (7932) and the amount they are sending up to $300.

For each Money Gram Express payment transaction, the following information must be provided:
a. Valid Inmate 8-digit register number (entered with no spaces or dashes), followed immediately by the Inmate's Last Name.
b. Company Name: Federal Bureau of Prisons
c. City and State: Washington, D.C.
d. Receive Code: Must always be 7932
e. Committed Inmate Full Name entered on Beneficiary Line

COMMISSARY FUND WITHDRAWALS

Inmates are allowed to send funds from their Commissary account to any recipient they choose. This can be accomplished in two ways:
1. Using a BP-199 form - Through TRULINCS, inmates can request to send money and fill out a BP-199 electronically by going to the "Manage Funds" option. After completing the application, print the form and give it to his or her Counselor for approval. Then a check will be cut to the recipient listed on the BP-199.
2. Through Money Gram via TRULINCS - Select the "Manage Funds" option to send money to anyone who is approved on the email contact list. Money can be sent up to $100.00 per day. Each transaction is a $4.95 fee. Money sent through Money Gram is available immediately for pick up. Be sure to include the correct address of the recipient. If you send money utilizing the wrong address, and your contact actually lives in a different state, the money will not be released. In that case, you have to wait a full 30 days for the funds to be returned to your account.

Now that you understand the basics of Commissary and how to receive money in your inmate account, let's discuss how to survive off of prison food. I had the pleasure of being housed with an incredible woman whom I consider to be an expert in the prison food department. She will inform you on what you need to know about prison food and provide some helpful hints.

SURVIVING OFF OF PRISON FOOD: FROM A PRISON HEAD COOK'S PERSPECTIVE

By: Renese Flowers

My name is Renese Flowers. I am currently the Head Cook at the Danbury Federal Prison Camp. I have been asked to share with you my insight on the BOP Food Service Department and provide a few tips about cooking in prison, which I've gained during my 5 years of incarceration.

Although it has been a difficult journey for me, leaving behind my daughter who is now 25 years old and my son who is 23 years old, I've tried my best to utilize my time in prison productively. Searching for ways to help pass time, I was extremely excited to learn I could participate in the Culinary Arts Apprenticeship, because I always enjoyed preparing food for my family and friends.

When I arrived at the Federal Prison Camp at Danbury, I worked in the kitchen for about a year. Shortly after, I applied for the Culinary Apprenticeship, which was offered inside the FCI when it was a women's facility. Through an intensive four month program, I participated in rigorous work groups learning the basics of bakery, lunch, dinner, appetizers, beverages and salad preparation. We received hands-on training preparing meals for the prison staff and waiting on them in the Officer's Mess Hall. Not only did I learn various skills that I'll be able to use for a life time, I was also awarded a certificate from the Department of Labor for completing the Cooking Apprenticeship. This accomplishment gave me the desire to pursue a career, and further my training in Culinary Arts when I exit prison this coming February.

After I completed my Apprenticeship at the FCI, I returned to the Camp where I was given a Grade One position as Head Cook. From my experience in this position, I will share with you the basics of what you should expect from prison food.

Food in Federal prison is generally decent. Many cooks, like myself, take pride in what we do. Because we are also inmates, we desire to take care of our own. In the Camp we have a little more flexibility because there are less people to feed. I personally take my time preparing and seasoning each dish as if I were serving it to my family at home. As a Southerner, serving tasty meals is extremely gratifying. Hopefully the Head Cook in the facility where you are housed will feel the same!

Throughout all BOP institutions there is uniformity in the food that is served, established by the BOP national menu, which requires institution wide adherence.

There are four national menus each BOP facility has to choose from, which are updated annually. The national menus have a five week schedule that are rotated. So you may get very tired of seeing the exact same food for months on end. The current budget is $1.60 per inmate per meal. Based on the budget, the Food Service Supervisor has the difficult job of purchasing food. According to the national menu and food availability, the institution menu is established by the Supervisor. (See Weekly National Menu at the conclusion of this chapter).

You should expect a combination of fresh and canned vegetables every day. The national menu I have worked with calls for two fresh fruits per day, but you may expect some of that to be canned and several days of only canned fruit. Salads are not offered regularly on the national menu, but your facility may offer salad more often if the Supervisor decides to work it into their budget.

You will be offered plenty of potatoes, white rice and beans. Rice may be flavored on occasions when Spanish entrees are offered. On some days either oven fried potatoes and heart healthy baked potatoes will be offered. Along with the main course, there will always be a protein alternative even if it is sometimes only a slice of processed American cheese.

The beverages on the national menu are not extensive, but you may at least expect to be offered coffee and milk at breakfast along with sugar and artificial sweetener. Also expect flavored and colored water at lunch and dinner. According to the national menu you will be offered a dessert, either baked or jello/pudding every other day. Some prisons may offer dessert more regularly.

There is frequently a difference in the way people approach the food when they first get to prison. Self surrenders tend to lose weight as they have been at home over eating under stress and generally need to lose weight, which they do when faced with the limited choices in prison. On the other hand, the detained inmates coming from county jails and detention centers tend to gain weight, as the food there is more frequently inedible, therefore, they are glad to at least be able to recognize what they are being offered.

SPECIAL MEALS

For those who have special dietary needs such as food allergies or sensitivities, the BOP will only accommodate you if it is documented as a medical condition in your PSR. Even then you may be informed that your "medical diet" must be accomplished by "self selection," which means do not eat what will make you sick.

If your documented religion is Jewish or Muslim there is a dietary program called "Common Fare" available offering Koska and Hakla prepared foods. To qualify for Common Fare you must put in a Cop Out to the Chaplain and expect to be interviewed. It is my understanding the quality of Common Fare meals varies from prison to prison due to the fact that meals are purchased from local vendors and therefore must fit into the budget the Food Service Supervisor is working with.

COOKING IN MICROWAVES

Many of the longer term inmates will develop the habit of preparing some of their meals in the microwaves that are provided in the units. Securing time to cook at one of the few available microwaves can be very competitive and is a common source of fights. Nonetheless, it is a means of survival for many in prison.

Microwaveable bowls can be purchased from Commissary, as well as a variety of food for cooking. The following are three popular and creative meals made by inmates using the microwave with limited resources.

RECIPES

Nachos - Ingredients and Preparation: Tortilla chips, cheese, chili beans with beef or refried beans to which you could add chicken or mackerel, and onion, pepper and tomatoes if available. To make the cheese sauce, you should use milk, if available, or either non-dairy creamer or powdered milk (to which you will need to add water). Add whatever seasonings you have to the chili while you are heating it - Sazon, Adobo, garlic powder, onion powder, etc. You may decide to cook down the fresh vegetables if you don't like them raw. Assemble all ingredients in order of your choice with the cheese on top and enjoy!

Prison Potato Log - Ingredients and Preparation: Crunch up one bag of chips, any type or variety in the bag. You may add Sazon in the bag as you crunch. Add water until the crumbs clump up or mold together. Next you flatten out the molded chips inside the bag and flip it on to either a clean trash bag or parchment paper if you can get it. In one bowl, mix chicken or fish, onions, peppers if available then add your spices. Place the bowl in the microwave and cook for two minutes. Next, pour this cooked mix into the middle of the spread out chips mixture, add cheese, pepperoni or sausage and add cheese on top. Finally, fold up each side to overlap each other with the bag, which will look like a roll of bread, and twist the ends of the bag. Tie a knot at the end of both sides of the bag and tuck it underneath. It will be ready after cooked in the microwave for three minutes. May be served with rice.

Fried Rice - Ingredients and Preparation: Place a bag of rice in a bowl with either mayonnaise or oil - approximately 2 tablespoons. Cook for three minutes stirring occasionally. Add vegetables and spices, plus soy sauce and sweet & hot sauce to taste. Next you can add whatever meat or fish you wish. Finally, add water according to your rice package and cook until done. Enjoy!

CONCLUSION

Regardless of the prison you are housed in, expect to be served decent food. Every national holiday, inmates are treated to special dishes. On

F.P.C. DANBURY Commissary List: November 2014

PRICES ARE SUBJECT TO CHANGE WITHOUT NOTICE

Approved: H. Quay, Warden

NAME:_____ Register #_____ Work Assignment:_____

*Stamps: ___ .49 Cents (Single) | $9.80 (One Book) | $1.00 ___ | $0.02 ___ | $0.05 ___ | $0.63 ___ | (Total Limit: $9.80)

PHOTO TICKETS (max 4): ___ ($1.00 each)   COPY CARD (max 2): ___ ($6.50)

BRAS (limit 1)	HYGIENE (limit 2 each)	SHAMPOO (limit 2 total)	GROOMING AIDS (limit 1 each)
___ Hanes/JMS $9.90 - $18.45	___ Maxi Pad with Wings 5.15	___ Pantene (White) 6.25	___ Shower Cap 1.20
Mark Size _____	___ Summer Eve (Cloth) 3.10	___ Suave Green Apple 2.15	___ Hair Scrunchies (8-pk) 4.80
	___ Summer Eve (Wash) 4.70	___ VO5 Kiwi Lime 1.95	___ Wide Tooth Comb 1.45
___ SPORT BRA $20.15	___ Douche (2-pk) 2.75	___ Head & Shoulder 7.75	___ Bobby Pins (Large) 0.80
Circle Size: SM MED LRG XL	___ Tampax (Super) 5.40	___ Selsun Blue 8.95	___ Bobby Pins (Small) 0.90
	___ Panty Shields 2.15	___ Optimum Shampoo 5.05	___ Stretch Wave Cap 3.25
MISCELLANEOUS (limit 1 each)	___ Tampax (Regular) 5.30	CONDITIONER (limit 2 total)	___ Pumice Stone 1.90
___ Hangers (EACH) (4 Total) 0.30	DENTAL (limit 1 each)	___ Optimum Conditioner 5.05	___ Cuticle Clipper 5.85
___ Towel 11.65	___ Denture Cup 1.90	___ Suave Green Apple 2.15	___ Toenail Clipper 1.10
___ Washcloth 1.95	___ G.U.M.'s Dental Picks 2.65	___ Infusium 23 8.55	___ Tweezers 1.15
PANTIES/ (limit 1 total)	___ Un Waxed Dental Floss 1.60	___ VO5 Kiwi Lime 1.95	___ Nose Scissors 6.70
(SZ 5-8) $7.30 SZ ___	___ Toothbrush Holder 0.50	___ Pantene (White) 6.70	___ Emory Boards 0.90
(SZ 10-13) $10.00 SZ ___	___ Close Up Toothpaste 2.65	___ Optimum Breakage 8.45	___ Cotton Q-Tips 1.80
Circle Size: MED LRG X-LRG	___ Colgate Toothpaste 2.60	LOTION (limit 1 each)	___ White Hair Brush 1.45
___ Poncho 3.65	___ Aim Toothpaste 1.80	___ Tone Coco Butter Lotion 2.90	___ 5" Clincher Comb 5.15
___ Baseball Cap 6.50	___ Colgate Sensitive Toothpaste 4.25	___ Jergens Lotion 4.55	___ Headband (2pk) 3.90
SHORT SLEEVE T-SHIRT (limit 1)	___ Toothbrush (Med) 0.95	___ St. Ives Collagen Lotion 7.10	___ Ponytail Holders 3.20
___ SM - 3X $5.60	___ Toothbrush (Soft) 0.95	___ St. Ives Shea Lotion 7.10	___ Rubber Bands 0.75
Mark Size _____	___ Mouthwash 1.50	___ Palmers Coco Butter Lotion 5.15	BAGS (limit 1 each)
SHORTS (limit 1)	___ Colgate Mouthwash 5.05	___ Nivea Lotion 5.35	___ Grey Gym Bag 10.95
___ SM – XL $9.10	___ Fixodent 4.40		___ Small Green Bag 6.50
___ 3XL $10.40	___ Denture Cream 5.60	SKIN CARE (limit 1 each)	___ Clear Shave Bag 6.00
Mark Size _____	HAIR CARE (limit 1 each)	___ Clearasil Daily Face Wash 9.65	MAKE-UP (limit 1 each)
SOCKS (3 each total)	___ Black Gel 2.80	___ Palmers small coco-butter 5.80	___ Powder Fondation-Med. Dk 4.00
___ Long Socks 3.65	___ Infusium 23 7.75	___ Noxzema Face Wash 1.80	___ Powder Foundation– Dark 4.00
___ 1/4 Socks 1.65	___ Profectiv Relaxer 7.80	___ Oil of Olay Cream 12.30	___ Powder Foundation Gld.Tan 4.00
___ Ankle Socks (3/pk) 4.35	___ Hot Six Oil 6.85	___ Apricot Scrub Blemish 4.65	___ Gold Coral Lip Gloss 0.70
SWEATS (Limit 1 Pant/1 Shirt)	___ Organic Root Olive Oil 6.70	___ Apricot Scrub 4.65	___ Berry Brown Lip Gloss 0.70
(Pants) SM-3X $19.50	___ Pink Oil 5.50	___ Collagen Face Cream 6.20	___ Mauvey Lip Gloss 3.00
Mark Size _____	___ 3 Minute Miracle 6.05	___ Petroleum Jelly 1.65	___ Rustic Lip Gloss 3.00
(Shirts) SM-3X $16.80	___ Lotta Body 4.45	___ Baby Powder 1.90	___ Pink Affair Lip Gloss 3.00
Mark Size _____	___ Sulfur 8 6.10	___ Esoterica Cream 12.15	___ Mini Black Eyeliner Pencil 1.70
BOOTS (1 each)	___ Hair Food 2.70	___ Ambi Face Cream 5.90	___ Mini Brown Eyeliner Pencil 1.00
___ BLACK BOOTS $69.50	___ Queen Helene Gel 3.25	___ Neutrogena Face Soap 3.65	___ Wet & Wild Face-Sun Kiss 3.45
Mark Size _____	___ Cholesterol 3.55	___ Revita-Lift Face/Neck 12.70	___ Wet & Wild Face- Natural 3.45
___ Boot Laces (Black) 1.05	___ Soft & Beautiful Relaxer 9.05	___ Ambi Face Soap 2.30	___ Wet & Wild Mascara 1.70
SHOWER SHOE/SLIPPER (1 each)	___ Garnier Sculpting Gel 5.85	___ Sun Block 3.90(1)	___ Nail Polish Remover 1.50
FLIP FLOPS	___ IC Hair Polisher 5.25	___ Alba Sun Block 10.35(1)	
Circle Size: SM MED LRG 1.05	___ Optimum 3 N'1 5.30	___ Hand Sanitizer 1.60	WATCHES (limit 1 each)
RADIOS / MP-3 (limit 1 total)	___ Dr. Miracle Temple Growth 8.45		___ Timex Women's Watch 29.70
___ Sony SRP Radio 41.60	___ Dr. Miracle Breakage Cream 8.65	BOOK/STATIONERY (qty each)	___ Timex Men's Watch 20.00
___ Sport MP3 Player 88.40	___ Mango Lock Twist 6.40	___ Phone Book 2.45(1)	
___ Old MP3 Cover 2.60	SOAP (limit 2 total/1 of each kind)	___ Photo Album 3.15(1)	HOBBY CRAFTS (limit 1 each)
___ Sport MP3 Cover 3.25	___ Dove Soap (Single) 1.85	___ Pencils (4-pk) 0.55(3)	___ Fluff Fill 5.20
	___ Ivory Soap (3-pk) 1.80	___ Envelope (Box) 1.80(3)	
Occasion Cards 0.55	___ Pure Soap (3-pk) 1.75	___ Typewriter Ribbon 7.65(3)	HEADPHONES (limit 1 each)
Missing You _____	___ Dial Soap (3-pk) 3.00	___ Envelope (Big/Yellow) 0.20(3)	___ Skull Candy Ear Buds 22.50
	___ Irish Spring Soap (3-pk) 3.05	___ Bic Pen (2/pk) 1.10(3)	___ Koss Headphone 35.00
Thinking Of You _____	___ Pure Cocoa Butter Soap(3pk) 1.75	___ Writing Pad 1.05(3)	
Anniversary _____	___ Healing Garden Body Wash 3.00	___ Notebook 1.70(3)	EYEWEAR (limit 1 total)
Love _____	___ St. Ives Body Wash 3.65	___ Spa / Eng dict 2.25	___ Reading Glasses 5.99-7.80
Thank you _____	___ Soap Dish 0.70	OTHER (limit 1 each)	Circle Size: 1.25- 1.75- 2.0- 2.25- 3.0
Friendship _____	___ Pomegranate Body Wash 5.00	___ Flatware (4-piece) 1.30	___ Sunglasses 5.25
	SHAVE (limit 1 each)	___ Mug 2.25	
Juvenile /Adult Birthday _____	___ Persona Comfort Razor 1.50	___ Water Bottle 2.95	LOCKS (limit 1 total)
	___ Bic Soleil Razors (4-pk) 8.35	___ Plastic Bowl 3.95	___ Combination Lock 5.90
Sympathy Card _____	___ Gillette Razors 8.90	___ Mirror 2.75	
		___ Ajax Dish Detergent 1.55	FRAGRANCE OIL (limit 1 total)
Spanish	DEODORANTS (limit 1 total)	___ Black Ice Air Freshener 1.50	
Love _____	___ Degree 3.00	___ Vanilla Air Freshener 1.50	___ Fragrance/Oils 3.90
	___ Suave 1.95	___ Sewing Kit 1.95	
Friendship _____	___ Secret 1.80	___ Locker Buddy 8.45	

OTC MEDICINES (Qty Each)

Item	Price
Chapstick Lip Balm	2.00(1)
Carmex Lip Balm	1.80(1)
Dr. Sch Gel Insert	14.30(1)
Comfort Insole	2.35(1)
Nasal Strips	2.75(1)
Tolfinate	7.50(1)
Clotrimazole Cream	3.10(1)
Gold Bond Foot Powder	5.20(1)
Foot Powder	1.50(1)
Midol	6.50(1)
Miconazole	10.60(2)
Vagisil	5.60(2)
Acne Treatment Cream	1.60(1)
Band-Aids	0.90(1)
Antibiotic Cream	4.75(1)
Hemorrhoid Cream	1.30(1)
Pepto-Bismol	2.40(1)
Gas-X	3.20(1)
Fiber	7.20(2)
Milk of Magnesia	2.25(1)
Laxative	1.70(1)
Anti-Diarrheal	3.25(1)
Tums (3-pk)	2.30(2)
Ranitidine	2.45(1)
Advance Ultrex Plus	3.75(1)
Vitamin B-Complex	2.95(2)
Vitamin C	2.95(2)
Calcium Tab	2.10(2)
Vitamin E	2.85(2)
Aspirin	1.65(1)
Pain/Naproxen	2.95(1)
Ibuprofen	2.65(1)
Non Aspirin	2.35(1)
Claritin	1.90(1)
CTM's ALLERGY	1.30 (1)
Allergy Eye Drops	2.15(1)
Cough Syrup	2.45(1)
Halls w/ Lemon	2.05(1)
Halls Sugar Free	2.05(1)
Chest Rub	2.10(2)
Saline Mist/Nasal	1.85(2)
Muscle Rub	2.00(2)
Cortizone Cream	1.60(1)
Generic Excedrine	3.70(1)
Orajel Tooth Pain Relief	1.60(1)
Omeprezole	14.50(1)
Dairy Digestive	11.40(1)
Artificial Tears	2.15(1)

RECREATION (quantity each)

Item	Price
Playing Cards	2.60(2)
Pinochle Cards	1.70(2)
Puzzle Books	2.00(2)

ELECTRICAL (limit 1 each)

Item	Price
Fan	14.95
O2 Cool Fan	32.50
Book Light	9.75
Alarm Clock	10.50

BATTERIES (limit 2 each)

Item	Price
AA	1.60
D Battery	2.55
AAA	1.60
Watch Battery	2.60

*Battery Number _____

Battery Number's 2016, 1216, 1620, 025, 1616 will be in stock, all other sizes must be requested by cop-out.

CHIPS (limit 2 each / 6 total)

Item	Price
Tortillas Chips	2.05K
Party Mix	2.35
Sour Cream & Onion	1.60K/H
Ripple Chips	1.60K/H
Plantain Chips	1.65
Sha-Bang Potato Chips	1.60
Nacho Chips	2.30

RICE/TORTILLAS (limit 2 each)

Item	Price
Long Grain Rice (5 ea)	1.15K/H
Brown Rice	1.35K/H
Flour Tortillas	1.60 K/H
Wheat Tortillas	2.00K

PASTA/PIZZA (limit 2 each)

Item	Price
Macaroni & Cheese	1.50K/H
Pizza Kit	3.65
Angel Hair Pasta	1.25
Ziti	1.15

SNACKS (limit 2 each)

Item	Price
Vanilla Pudding	1.95K
Peanut Butter	2.95K
Microwave Popcorn	0.60(3)

PASTRY (limit 2 each)

Item	Price
Honey Bun	0.95K
Mini Donuts	2.85
Buddy Bars	2.10

CANDY (limit 4 bars ea & 2 bags ea)

Item	Price
Dove Dark Chocolate Bar	1.10
M&M's Peanut	1.10
Reeses Pieces	1.20
Hershey Kisses	1.95
Snickers	1.00
Hersey white choc	2.65
Vanilla Caramels	0.65
Fireballs	0.70
Now & Later	0.80
Jolly Rancher	1.55
Peppermints	1.15
Sugar Free Jolly Rancher	2.45
Sugar Free Wild Fruit	0.75
Strawberry Chocolate Bar	2.55
Chocolate Peanut Clusters	1.50
Certs	0.75
Tootsie Pops	1.45

COOKIES (limit 2 total)

Item	Price
Vanilla Wafers	2.20K/H
Animal Crackers	1.85K
Pecan Cookies Bag	1.05
Oreo's 6 pk	.50
Famous Amous cookies	.55

SOUPS (limit 24 total)

Item	Price
Cajun Shrimp Soup (Bag)	0.25
Vegetable Soup (Cup)	0.50
Thai Noodle Soup (Bag)	0.65
Ramen Chicken Soup (Bag)	0.25
Ramen Beef Soup (Bag)	0.25

MEATS (limit 10 total)

Item	Price
Halal Summer Sausage	2.45
Pepper Turkey Log	1.80
Spam Singles	1.60
Chicken Pouch	3.90
Chili W/Beans	1.75
Beef Deli Stick	1.65
Pepperoni Slices	2.35
Vienna Sausage	2.00
Beef Summer Sausage	1.85

CONDIMENTS (limit 1 each)

Item	Price
Ketchup	1.85K
Mayonnaise	2.90K
Sweet &Hot Sauce	1.80
Soy Sauce	1.55K
Louisiana Hot Sauce	1.40
Chili Garlic Sauce	1.95K
Mrs. Dash Table Blend	3.15
Mrs. Dash Caribbean	3.15
Cilantro Cubes	1.90
Sazon	1.60
Goya Adobo	1.90
Onion Powder	1.55K
Garlic Powder	1.25K
Veggie Flakes	1.35K
Pasta Sauce	0.60
BBQ Sauce	2.05
Chicken Bouillion Cubes	1.70
True Lemon	4.40
Grated Italian Cheese	1.70
Salt and Pepper	2.35

HEALTH FOODS (Quantity each)

Item	Price
Oatmeal fruit n cream	3.15(1)
Instant Breakfast	7.00K(1)
Plain Oatmeal	2.75(1)
Honey Nut Granola Bag	300(1)
Caramel Rice Cakes	3.40(2)
Honey&Oat Granola Bar	0.50(6)
Sweet /Salty Almond Bar	0.65(6)
Red Berries Cereal Bar	0.70(6)
Honey & Oat Cereal	2.60(1)
Honey Nut Scooters	3.10(1)
Cinnamon Toasters	3.10(1)
Honey Wheat Pretzels	3.45(2)
Cookies&Cream Crunch	1.80(3)
Peanut Butter Bar	1.55(3)
*Caramel Crunch**	1.55(3)
Balanced Nutrition Bar	

KOSHER/HALAL (Limit 2 each)

Item	Price
Hummus	4.80K/H
Chicken Mush. Meal	5.05/H
Beef Cholent Meal	7.90K/H
Chicken Noodle Cup Soup	1.80K
Refried Beans	2.20K/H
Gefite Fish Meal	5.20K

PRODUCE (limit 3 each)

Item	Price
Pickle	0.70K
Hot Pickle	0.70K
Jalapeno Pepper	1.95K/H
Green Olives	1.20K
Four Cheese Mash Potato	1.50K
Black Beans	1.30K
Goya	2.55K
Unsalted Saltine	2.60K/H
Graham Crackers	2.50
Cheese Crackers	2.80
Snack Crackers	3.20

DAIRY (Quantity each)

Item	Price
Velveeta Jalapeno tub	1.80(2)
Velveeta Cheddar pack	0.60(6)
City Cow Mozzarella stick	1.60(2)
Shredded Mozzarella pack	0.90(4)

FISH (limit 14 each)

Item	Price
Tuna	1.65K/H
Mackerel	1.15K/H
Sardines in Tomato Sauce	1.05
Albacore Tuna	2.25
Salmon Flakes in Water	2.00

NUTS (limit 2 each)

Item	Price
Almonds	4.05K
Honey Roasted Peanuts	0.80
Mixed Nuts	3.10
Salted Nuts	0.60
Unsalted Nuts	2.80

SWEETENERS (limit 1 total)

Item	Price
Splenda (box)	3.75K
Honey	3.55K
Sweet&Low (box)	3.00

DRINKS (limit 12 each)

Item	Price
Water	0.55
Soy Milk (3-pk)	9.05K

MIXES/TEAS (limit 2 ea)

Item	Price
Kool-Aid Punch	2.15K/H
Tang	2.25K/H
Peach Drink	2.15K/H
Gatorade Frost	0.75
Bigelow Assorted Herb Tea	3.35
Celestial Assorted Herb Tea	3.00
Nestea Box Tea	4.80K
Peach Tea Box (8/pk)	1.55

COFFEE/COCOA (limit each)

Item	Price
Columbian Coffee	3.60
Tasters Choice	4.80K
Coffee Singles	0.15(10)
Plain Creamer	1.70K
Decaffeinated Coffee	3.55K
Sugar Free Cocoa (Box)	1.80
French Vanilla Creamer	3.70K
Regular Cocoa (Bag)	1.80
Cappucino	1.75K
Instant Milk (Box)	4.30

SODA (LIMIT TWO 12pk)

Item	Price
Pepsi	6.10
Diet Pepsi	6.10
Ginger Ale	6.10
Orange Crush	1.20

ICE CREAM (limit 1 total)

Item	Price
Butter Pecan Ice Cream	2.30
Wildberry Frozen Yogurt	1.40
Creamy Vanilla Ice Cream	2.30
Moose Track Cone	1.55
Cookies & Cream Cone	0.90

RELIGIOUS ITEMS (*must have signed cop-out by Rel. Services)

Item	Price
Black Hijab	$11.99
Black Two-Piece Hijab	$7.99
Off-White Hijab	$11.99

HAIR DYE/RINSE (limit 1 total)

Item	Price
Black Hair Dye	$3.75
Blonde Hair Dye	$3.75
Brown Hair Dye	$3.75
Auburn Hair Dye	$3.60
Clairol Black Rinse	$9.45
Clairol Brown Rinse	$9.45
Clairol Blonde Rinse	$9.45
Bigen Black Rinse	$3.75
Bigen Cognac Rinse	$3.75
Bigen Blonde Rinse	$3.75

YARN (limit 2 each)

CROCHET:

Item	Price
White Crochet Thread	$4.10
Natural Crochet Thread	$4.10

ACRYLIC:

Item	Price
White Acrylic	$3.20
Natural Acrylic	$3.20
Shades of brn	$3.30
Aspen Mist	$3.30

Balanced Nutrition Bar

Menu Type: Mainline FY 2015

Weekly Menu

Week #: 1 Date Range: _____

Sunday	Monday	Tuesday	Wednesday	Thursday	Friday	Saturday
BREAKFAST	**BREAKFAST**	**BREAKFAST**	**BREAKFAST**	**BREAKFAST**	**BREAKFAST**	**BREAKFAST**
^Bran Flakes ♥	^Hot Oatmeal ♥	^Hot Grits ♥	^Hot Oatmeal ♥	^Hot Grits ♥	^Hot Oatmeal ♥	^Bran Flakes ♥
^Breakfast Cake or	Creamed Beef	Breakfast Cake or	Pancakes	Breakfast Cake or	French Toast (2)	Breakfast Cake or
^Whole Wheat Bread ♥	Oven Brown Potatoes or	^Whole Wheat Bread ♥	W/Syrup or	^Whole Wheat Bread ♥	W/Syrup or	^Whole Wheat Bread ♥
and ^Jelly (2) ♥	^Boiled Potatoes ♥	and ^Jelly (2) ♥	^Whole Wheat Bread ♥	and ^Jelly (2) ♥	^Whole Wheat Bread ♥	and ^Jelly (2) ♥
^Sugar Substitute Pks ♥	^Sugar Substitute Pks ♥	^Sugar Substitute Pks ♥	and ^Jelly (2) ♥	^Sugar Substitute Pks ♥	and ^Jelly (2) ♥	^Sugar Substitute Pks ♥
^Margarine Pat ♥	Biscuits (2) or	^Margarine Pat ♥	^Sugar Substitute Pks ♥	^Margarine Pat ♥	^Sugar Substitute Pks ♥	^Margarine Pat ♥
^Fresh Apple ♥	^Whole Wheat Bread ♥	^Fresh Apple ♥	^Margarine Pat ♥	^Fresh Apple ♥	^Margarine Pat ♥	^Fresh Apple ♥
^Coffee ♥	and ^Jelly (2) ♥	^Coffee ♥	^Fresh Bananas ♥	^Coffee ♥	^Fresh Bananas ♥	^Coffee ♥
^Skim Milk ♥	^Margarine Pat ♥	^Skim Milk ♥	^Coffee ♥	^Skim Milk ♥	^Coffee ♥	^Skim Milk ♥
	^Fresh Apple ♥		^Skim Milk ♥		^Skim Milk ♥	
	^Coffee ♥					
	^Skim Milk ♥					
LUNCH	**LUNCH**	**LUNCH**	**LUNCH**	**LUNCH**	**LUNCH**	**LUNCH**
^Plain Omelet ♥	Hot Dogs (2)	Chicken Patty Sandwich	^Hamburger ♥	^Baked Chicken ♥	Breaded Fish Sand or	Klebasa Sausage
^Oven Brown Potatoes ♥	#or Soy Burger ♥	#or Soy Chicken Patty ♥	#or Soy Burger	#or PB & Jelly Sand (2)	^Baked Fish ♥	#or Cottage Cheese ♥
Salsa	Tater Tots or	^Italian Pasta Salad ♥	Sliced Cheese	^Steamed Rice ♥	#or Soy Burger w/	^Boiled Potatoes ♥
Cream Gravy	^Baked Potato ♥	^Lett/Tom/Onion ♥	French Fries or	^Pinto Beans ♥	Salad Dressing	^Simmered Cabbage ♥
Biscuits (2) or	^Coleslaw ♥	^Carrots ♥	^Baked Potato ♥	^Green Beans ♥	^Macaroni Salad ♥	^Carrots ♥
^Whole Wheat Bread ♥	Catsup & Mustard	Salad Dressing	^Shredded Lettuce ♥	^Whole Wheat Bread ♥	^Green Peas ♥	Mustard
and ^Jelly (2) ♥	Hot Dog Buns (2) or	Hamburger Bun or	Catsup & Mustard	^Margarine Pat ♥	Hamburger Bun or	^Whole Wheat Bread ♥
^Margarine Pat ♥	^Whole Wheat Brd (2) ♥	^Whole Wheat Brd (2) ♥	Pickles	Dessert or	^Whole Wheat Brd (2) ♥	^Margarine Pat ♥
^Fruit ♥	^Margarine Pat ♥	^Margarine Pat ♥	Salad Dressing	^Fruit ♥	^Margarine Pat ♥	Dessert or
^Beverage	^Fruit ♥	Dessert or	Hamburger Bun or	^Beverage	Tartar Sauce	^Fruit ♥
	^Beverage	^Fruit ♥	^Whole Wheat Brd (2) ♥		^Fruit ♥	^Beverage
		^Beverage	^Margarine Pat ♥		^Beverage	
			^Fruit ♥			
			^Beverage			
DINNER	**DINNER**	**DINNER**	**DINNER**	**DINNER**	**DINNER**	**DINNER**
^Roast Beef ♥	^Vegetable Soup ♥	^Meatloaf ♥	Baked Turkey Ham	Beef Ench Casserole	Chicken Fried Rice ♥	^Spaghetti Pasta ♥
#or Cottage Cheese ♥	^Chicken Salad ♥	#or Soy Burger w/	# or BBQ Tofu ♥	^or Beef & Vegetables ♥	#or Tofu Fried Rice	^Meatsauce ♥
^Baked Potato ♥	#or Hummus ♥	Salad Dressing	^Baked Sweet Potato ♥	#or Soy Ench Casserole	^Steamed Broccoli ♥	#or Soy Spag Sauce
^Green Beans ♥	^Green Peas ♥	^Mashed Potatoes ♥	^Navy Beans ♥	^Steamed Rice ♥	^Whole Wheat Bread ♥	^Spinach ♥
^Black Eyed Peas ♥	^Potato Salad ♥	Tomato Gravy	^Collard Greens ♥	^Mixed Vegetables ♥	^Margarine Pat ♥	Garlic Bread or
Brown Gravy	^Lett/Tom/Onion ♥	WK Corn ♥	^Whole Wheat Bread ♥	^Whole Wheat Bread ♥	^Beverage	^Whole Wheat Bread ♥
^Whole Wheat Bread ♥	Pickles	^Whole Wheat Bread ♥	^Margarine Pat ♥	^Margarine Pat ♥		^Margarine Pat ♥
^Margarine Pat ♥	^Whole Wheat Brd (2) ♥	^Margarine Pat ♥	^Beverage	^Beverage		^Beverage
^Beverage	^Margarine Pat ♥	^Beverage				
	^Beverage					

* Indicates Pork.   # Indicates No Flesh Entree Item.   ^ Indicates Heart Healthy

Thanksgiving and Christmas Day the meals we receive are likened to feasts that are extremely enjoyable.

You will learn, just as I did, that you can do a lot with a very few ingredients. Therefore, be creative and think outside the box. Discover the prison meals you like the most and learn to prepare quick and easy meals that will sustain you. Before you know it, your prison journey will be over and you will once again enjoy and appreciate the luxuries of food in the free world!

KEY TERMS AND DEFINITIONS

BP-199 - The form inmates fill out to send money out of their Commissary account to a recipient of their choice.

COMMISSARY - The BOP store inmates shop at during designated days and times.

COMMON FARE - Special trays prepared for Muslim or Jewish inmates that meet Halal/Kosher standards.

LOCK BOX - The location where money orders and checks are received for all BOP inmates.

NATIONAL MENU - The menu followed in most every institution within the BOP. Meals are standardized based on this menu.

Chapter 8
Prison Politics 101

Prison Work Assignments and Duties

Shortly after an inmate completes A&O and is medically cleared, he or she must obtain a regular job assignment. Welcome to Prison Politics 101!

Working in prison has many tricky twists and turns. In this chapter, I will inform you about the basics of prison politics and teach you how to land a decent job while incarcerated.

Federal inmates are expected to work 7 hours per day, five days a week. In most Federal institutions, inmate jobs help to facilitate the orderly running of the facility. Without the large inmate work force within most prison institutions, the facilities would not receive the proper maintenance and service necessary to run effectively. Therefore, inmate jobs are often considered a big deal to inmates as well as staff.

As in the outside world, your job in prison is seen by others as a sign of stature. The difference is that you are not in control of your career as you would be in the outside world. Imagine Michael Vick, (NFL professional football player) working as a janitor or Martha Stewart, (celebrity home stylist) scrubbing bathrooms. No matter your affluence, once you become a Federal inmate, you have little power over how you will spend a great deal of your time in prison.

For most, the best jobs in prison are "desk jobs" or those that require little physical labor. Each department has inmates who are paid on grade levels one through four, in accordance with Inmate Performance Pay (IPP). Inmates are paid between $0.12 - $0.40 per hour based on their pay grade. The inmate with the highest grade in each department is generally labeled the Clerk. He or she handles the paperwork and typically supervises the functions of other inmates in the department.

Clerks are heavily relied upon by their BOP supervisor. In many cases, the clerk becomes very influential among inmates and other staff members because they generally call the shots on what happens within the department. As a result, the clerk positions are highly sought after by inmates. It generally takes several years to become a clerk, unless a position comes open and there is no one else to fill it. This is because you have to prove yourself to the BOP supervisor.

Now with an understanding of the basics, it is essential for you to know that in order to get a good job you MUST seek the assistance of others who work in the department you wish to work. Your best contact will be made with the inmate Clerk. If he or she recommends you for the job, you are more likely to get it. Likewise, if he or she disapproves, chances are you will be blocked from getting that job.

It is my suggestion, once you have settled in, you immediately ask around about jobs and begin to network with those who are in the department you wish to work. Once you find a department to accept you, ask the Foreman to sign a Cop Out which states you wish to work for their department. Be friendly and do not step on toes. Remember the rules of prison politics; inmates technically run the jobs within the prison. Therefore, go to the Clerk directly, be humble and ask what openings their department has available. Then ask if he or she will assist you with getting the job.

When you land a position, remain humble and do not try to show off your talent too much. Many inmates are insecure. If you come into their department and attempt to steal their shine, they will do their best to get you fired. This will make your work environment unbearable, which will ultimately cause your prison stay to be miserable. Therefore, always be pleasant and courteous, especially to those with whom you work.

JOB DESIGNATION

The Counselor designates job assignments to all inmates. After A&O, if you do not have a Cop Out signed by a Foreman, the Counselor will automatically place you in any job that is open. This can be dangerous! Once you are assigned to a job, you are generally stuck there. Therefore, be proactive, and do your best to find a job you desire. Since much of your time in prison will be spent working, it is worth your while to seek out employment you will be content with.

INSTITUTIONAL JOBS

Institutional jobs vary according to the needs of each institution. As discussed, inmates are generally expected to work 7 hours a day, 5 days a week. But, certain jobs require substantially less work time. For instance, orderlies generally clean a couple hours a day, which leaves them substantial free time. There are also weekend orderly jobs available at many institutions, which require light work.

At the Danbury Prison Camp where I am housed, the lighter jobs are inside of the Camp in departments such as Recreation, Education, Religious Services and the Kitchen. In these departments, after an inmate performs their assigned duties, they are free for the rest of the day. On the other hand, inmates who work outdoors, in departments such as Grounds, Out Electric, Plumbing, Construction, UNICOR and Warehouse, are required to stay at their work sites the entire day. Accordingly, inside jobs are generally more desirable in a Camp setting, unless you are relying on the pay to support yourself.

The key to finding a comfortable position is to speak to others and seek out employment opportunities. Below I will list the common jobs and duties for federal inmates so you can get an idea of what jobs are available:

EDUCATION - Jobs in Education include tutoring, teaching GED students, teaching Adult Continuing Education (ACE) classes, Career Center Technician and Library clerks. Education jobs are normally highly sought out, as they encompass meaningful work. People who work in the Education Department generally enjoy their jobs. Therefore, these positions are often unavailable until an inmate worker is released.

KITCHEN - Jobs in Food Service include: Cook, Baker, Server, Dishroom Attendant, Table and Floor cleaners, Trash attendant, Maintenance, Salad Prep and Clerk. Kitchen workers prepare food, cook, serve and clean for 3 meals daily. These are the most labor intensive jobs inside the facility. However, there are definitely benefits for the hard work such as obtaining extra food including fresh fruit or vegetables.

ORDERLY - Orderlies clean certain areas within the facility. These areas include: bathrooms, units, common areas and the visiting room. Although an orderly does not work a typical 7 hour day, they are often called to complete random tasks such as unloading a truck of supplies, moving lockers or overnight snow removal.

LAUNDRY - Jobs in laundry involve the collection of inmate and shop laundry bags, washing and drying clothes, distributing laundry and "dressing out" A&O inmates. Laundry jobs are highly sought after as they allow independent work and extra washing privileges.

WAREHOUSE/COMMISSARY - Includes loading, unloading, stocking Commissary items, and keeping track of inventory. Working in the warehouse or Commissary involves heavy lifting and climbing, as well as factory inventory skills. Additionally, on designated Commissary days, workers fill and prepare inmate Commissary baskets. Although warehouse and Commissary workers generally have many duties, they are paid very well through the Inmate Trust Fund. Outside of UNICOR workers, typically Commissary workers are paid the highest wages within the institution.

RECREATION AIDE - Aides in recreation are responsible for the maintenance of all recreation areas and equipment including the outdoor track, fitness center and recreation room. They are also responsible for assisting with recreation classes, special events and holiday events. Once a week, Recreation Aides assist staff with the hobby craft program, which is the mail out service for inmates who complete handmade craft projects that are mailed to family and friends. Recreation jobs are generally laid back and highly sought after.

CONSTRUCTION/MAINTENANCE SERVICES (CMS) - Commonly referred to as the "shops" includes Construction, Maintenance, Electric, Paint, Plumbing, Safety, Woodworking, Welding and HVAC shops where foremen train and teach inmates in these trades. Inmates who work in these areas generally cover the maintenance of the entire institution, making them highly relied upon. Typical CMS jobs require a lot of work. Also, inmates in these areas work a full seven hour day.

GROUNDS - In a Camp facility, grounds workers are second only to food service in number of employees. They are responsible for landscaping, grass cutting, shrubbery trimming, planting and snow removal. If you're serving a short sentence during the Spring and Summer and enjoy the outdoors, this is an ideal job for you. Otherwise, expect to be part of one of the hardest working crews in the Camp as Grounds jobs require a strong work ethic.

COMPOUND CLEANING SERVICE (CCS) A.M./P.M. - At higher security facilities, the Compound Cleaning Service or "Yard" workers maintain the landscaping of the prison grounds and pick up trash. This is typically a light job because there isn't much work to do except during snowstorms. The shifts for these workers are divided by a.m., 6 a.m. to 2 p.m. and p.m., 2 p.m. to 8 p.m. Generally this is an ideal job for someone who doesn't want to do too much work.

FEDERAL PRISON INDUSTRY (FPI) - Also know as UNICOR, is a wholly owned subsidiary of the U.S. Government, which runs factories and service centers at many federal prisons. These prison factories help produce office furniture, electronics, plastics, clothing, textiles, industrial products and military equipment and provide services such as telemarketing sales. All products and services provided by UNICOR are only sold to Federal departments and agencies, Government institutions and their authorized contractors or representatives.

These jobs are typically the highest paid within the institution. Inmates are paid between $0.23 to $1.35 per hour, according to their pay grade. UNICOR workers can earn up to $300 per month, thereby making these jobs highly sought after and desired by inmates.

UNICOR - UNICOR workers can earn up to $300.00 per month, thereby making these jobs highly sought after and desired by inmates.

APPRENTICESHIP PROGRAMS - Accredited apprenticeship programs are available in most federal prisons. These apprenticeships include: furniture repair/cabinet making, electrical repair, horticulture, plumbing, carpentry, tailoring, cooking/baking, data entry, computer operation, recreation aide, education aide, and other skills/trades. Upon the completion of six to forty-eight months of training, amounting to a total of 2000 to 8000 hours with an average of 2000 hours of hands-on and academic training per year, inmates earn an apprenticeship certificate through the Department of Labor. Inmates are typically encouraged by the Foreman of their department to participate in apprenticeships that are awarded in their particular area.

INMATE PAY

All inmates are paid once a month by the BOP. As previously discussed, inmates are paid on a grade level of one to four, one being the highest pay. In accordance with the IPP, inmates are paid $0.12 - $0.40 per hour based on their pay grade, which averages between $16.80 - $56.00 a month, without bonuses.

Inmates who perform minimal duties are given Maintenance Pay. It is the lowest wages which any working inmate can receive. Currently, maintenance pay is $5.25/monthly. Inmates who perform well can have their pay level increased, except inmates who do not possess a high school diploma or GED. Inmates who do not have a GED are automatically classified under the lowest pay grade, level four.

INMATE FINANCIAL RESPONSIBILITY PROGRAM (FRP)

The BOP, working with the Courts and the Department of Justice, administers a systematic payment program for court-ordered restitution, fines, fees and costs. All designated inmates are required to develop a financial plan to meet their financial obligations.

Based on the inmate's financial obligations and incoming funds (including pay wages and gifts), Case Managers set a required payment schedule. Unless a court order is in place that obligates the inmate to pay the minimum payment, which is $25.00 per quarter, inmates who have restitution or fines will be required to pay up to 50 percent of everything they receive each month above $75.00. This monthly payment requirement can become quite hefty. Therefore, inmates who have large fines and restitution should monitor their incoming funds. The more money the inmate receives, the more they will be required to pay.

Shortly after an inmate completes A&O, he or she is required to develop a plan for repayment of restitution, fines, fees, costs and obligations in conjunction with their Case Manager. The inmate signs documentation taking full responsibility for compliance in making monthly or quarterly payments either from their prison job earnings or outside sources. If an inmate fails at any time to meet their financial obligations, they may be placed in "refusal" status. Sanctions imposed as a result of being in "refusal" status include, but are not limited to:

- Termination or denial of employment at UNICOR
- Placement in less desirable housing
- Monthly Commissary spending limit of $25.00 or less
- Placement on maintenance pay - $5.25/monthly
- Inability to be considered for favorable requests such as job vacations, furloughs, programs or early releases

The status of an inmate's financial plan is included in all Progress Reports and will be considered by staff when considering job assignments and participation in programs.

Now that you understand the basics of prison jobs and prison politics, you will be able to utilize this information to gain a decent prison job and sustain your peace while incarcerated. Once you land your desired position, be sure to value it. Show up on time, be courteous and complete your work assignments. If not, you will jeopardize losing what you've worked hard to gain.

KEY TERMS AND DEFINITIONS

COMPOUND CLEANING SERVICE (CCS) - The maintenance of the prison grounds, landscaping and trash pick up jobs in higher security institutions.

CONSTRUCTION MAINTENANCE SERVICE (CMS) - Construction, Maintenance, Electric, Paint, Plumbing, Safety, Woodworking, Welding and HVAC shops in minimum security facilities.

FEDERAL PRISON INDUSTRY (FPI) AKA UNICOR - A wholly owned subsidiary of the U.S. Government that runs factories and service centers at many Federal prisons, employing Federal inmates.

FOREMAN - The direct supervisor of inmates for a particular department within a facility.

INMATE FINANCIAL RESPONSIBILITY PROGRAM (FRP) - A systematic inmate payment program for court-ordered restitution, fines, fees and court costs.

INMATE PERFORMANCE PAY (IPP) - The four levels of pay that inmates receive from grade one through four, which is based on inmate performance.

MAINTENANCE PAY - The minimum pay an inmate can receive for his or her services. Currently the rate is $5.25 per month.

REFUSAL STATUS - The status of an inmate who fails to meet their financial obligation for monthly or quarterly repayment of restitution, fines, fees and costs.

Chapter 9
Leisure Time and Recreation

Making the Best Out of Time
By: Jamila T. Davis

Keeping your sanity and maintaining your peace in prison depends on how you utilize your leisure time. The more you stay idle, the more time you will have to think about all the things you are missing out on. Therefore, it is my suggestion that you try your best to stay as busy as possible. Unlike in the outside world, you will not have many tools to keep your mind occupied, so you will have to create things to do.

To date, I have served over 6 1/2 years behind bars. I never dreamed I would be able to survive such a lengthy sentence, yet I have! Since I've been incarcerated, I have completed my degree, written several books and participated in numerous recreational and educational programs. Currently, I hold the position as Clerk of the Recreation Department at the Danbury Federal Prison Camp. Utilizing my personal experience, in this chapter I will share survival tips with you on how to make the best out of time!

Your prison sentence does not have to be the worst experience of your life. It can be a place for you to regroup, plan how to live prosperously and maintain great health, which will be useful for the rest of your life. Take advantage of the time you've been given by working on your greatest asset - yourself!

In the free world, I was consistently on the go. With meetings, caring for my children and maintaining my social status in the community, I had little time to take care of my body. In prison, I have been forced to slow down and take notice of what I neglected.

Look at your prison stay as a vacation and get some rest. You may never have an opportunity to sleep as much in your life. Take advantage of the rest and allow your body to heal from the heavy damage it may have encountered in the free world. It is not my suggestion you sleep your time away, which can lead to depression. Although, I do suggest you get lots of rest, it is also important to set goals and be productive.

Even though I am locked behind bars, I continue to keep a daily "Things to Do" list. I set goals regularly and I check off my accomplishments. This has kept me focused. I suggest you do the same. Do you desire to lose weight? Are you looking to make a career change? Do you want to learn new skills? Or, do you desire to participate in fun activities that will make your time fly by? If so, plan accordingly; take advantage of the programs the BOP offers. Use your time to increase your skills and look to meet people who can share knowledge about things you are interested in.

In this chapter I will share general information about the BOP Recreation programs as well as correspondence programs. Participating in these programs will not only help ensure you a smoother stay, they can empower you to have a productive future!

THE BOP RECREATION DEPARTMENT

The BOP encourages inmates to make constructive use of leisure time and offers group and individual activities. Through the Recreation Department leisure, wellness, sports and music programs are provided to promote positive lifestyle changes. They are designed to reduce stress and enhance overall health and emotional well-being.

Leisure programs include a wide variety of classes including hobby crafts, music, sports and games. Many of the leisure program classes are Sentry based, meaning inmates are awarded Sentry credit, which is reflected in their Progress Reports upon completion. The more an inmate participates in structured classes, the higher he or she is scored in rehabilitation. As a result, participation can reduce the security level of inmates.

At the Danbury Federal Prison Camp, most Sentry recreation classes are within the Art and Hobby Craft Programs. Inmates are taught how to crochet, knit, plastic canvas, cross stitch, draw, paint and create glass art. All required materials are supplied by the BOP for these classes, which are structured with a well written curriculum.

I've seen inmates make incredible projects after attending these recreational classes. I have also participated and learned to knit and crochet. At the Camp, many of us spend a substantial amount of time making hand crafted items for our family members. Completing these projects makes the time go by faster and helps us to sustain our peace.

Additionally, our Recreation Department has several Wellness programs. Inmates are encouraged to work out, eat properly and stay in shape. Through yoga, nutrition and other physical fitness programs such as Pilates and Circuit Training, inmates are provided a structured curriculum to maintain good health. At Danbury FPC, there is access to an amazing outdoor track and field that has a park ground, mountain side view, and a gym that is filled with up-to-date equipment.

I've personally witnessed inmates lose substantial weight participating in recreational activities. Once you get started, you won't want to stop!

All year round the Recreation Department has a variety of sports leagues, basketball, softball and volleyball teams that compete. Being part of one of those leagues or just watching them play is a good way to relax for many inmates.

In addition to sports and hobby crafts, the Recreation Department has music programs. At the Danbury FPC we have an amazing guitar class given on both a beginner and intermediate level. I never thought I'd learn to play the guitar, but I did! I was actually privileged to participate in the Intermediate Guitar class with Lauryn Hill, a multi-grammy award winning artist, who served a 3 month sentence at the Danbury FPC. Our class together turned into many jam sessions. I often forgot I was in prison as I listened to Lauryn play and sing as if she were performing live in concert.

The Recreation Department also facilitates holiday games and tournaments; spades, bridge, pinochle, cribbage, Guesstures, dominoes, bingo and outdoor tournaments. There are a variety of fun activities for inmates on the holidays. Winners are awarded prizes including hygiene products, picture tickets and candy bags. It may sound sort of childish, but behind bars, these activities are major fun!

During warm weather holidays, music is also played outdoors. You would be surprised how much inmates enjoy the sounds of music, which reminds them of life in the free world. Between outdoor activities and holiday events, we are provided a means of escape from the every day, mundane prison life.

Participation in recreation activities is not required, but I highly suggest getting involved. You will gain or discover talents you probably never suspected you had. It's an awesome way to pass time and a great escape in prison!

LEARNING IN PRISON

In the free world, I was often too busy to pick up a book. Prison has afforded me the ability to spend several hours reading about things I always wished to know. From behind bars, I've learned how to do many things, including self-publishing, just by reading books. You can do the same!

Take a minute to day dream and think about how you want your life to be when you get out of prison. Think about the profession you wish to have and the skills you wish to obtain. Then, ask your relatives to research these topics and send you books. I've found some wonderful, helpful books that have substantially increased my knowledge about many things I wish to do upon my release.

CORRESPONDENCE PROGRAMS

I always desired to complete my degree, but after I became a multi-millionaire at the age of 25, completing my education was no longer a priority. A little over three years into my incarceration, I decided to enroll in correspondence courses. My first correspondence program was through Rhema Bible School where I received a diploma in Religious Studies.

After I started this course, I became a life-long learner. I was so excited about how much I could learn through independent study. I would often get lost for hours completing each lesson, which not only helped me to gain more knowledge, but also increased my spiritual strength.

After this experience, I enrolled at Ashworth College, where I completed my Associate in Science degree in Psychology. Ashworth is accredited by the Distance Education Training Council (DETC), and is recognized by Government and private work force, and other civil service industries. I enjoyed the ease of the independent study program structure which was easy to follow and very convenient. For under $4,000, I was able to complete my Associate degree, through an affordable $49.00 a month payment program. I was able to maintain communication with the school through the FPC Education Department. Now Ashworth has a department that handles emails through Corrlinks for all their federally incarcerated students.

I am currently enrolled at the Newburgh Theological Seminary where I am studying to receive my Bachelor of Arts degree in Christian Education. Through this program I was able to read certain required books and write papers about what I learned to receive credit. Just like Ashworth, the school has affordable payment plans. For less than $2,000 out of pocket, I will have my Bachelor of Arts degree.

The next step for me is to enroll in law school. Yes, you read that right! I will be attending Northwestern California Law School next year to complete my Juris Doctorate degree through correspondence. With the requirement of having completed 60 credit hours, any student can enroll in their school. Just like Ashworth and Newburgh, Northwestern California Law School is affordable. For less than $10,000 through an affordable payment plan, I intend to complete my Juris Doctorate degree.

I was happy to learn in certain states, including California, felons can become licensed attorneys. I learned this information behind bars, by reading a book. Through my experience, I realized prison does not have to be a death sentence, even for a person like myself who is serving a decade plus sentence. Instead, I chose to use it as a platform for my biggest success - the next chapter of my life!

Why waste your time on pity and grief? Take back your freedom by controlling how you do your time. Take advantage of the recreation activities that are provided and consider enrolling in correspondence courses.

Below is a list of popular correspondence courses for inmates which I hope will assist you:

UNDERGRADUATE CORRESPONDENCE DEGREE PROGRAMS

Adams State College
208 Edgemont Boulevard
Alamosa, CO 81102
800-548-6679
www.adams.edu

Ashworth College
430 Technology Parkway
Norcross, GA 30092
800-640-9524
www.ashworthcollege.edu

Brigham Young University
Independent Study
120 Morris Center
Provo, UT 84602
www.byu.edu

Global University
1211 Glenstone Avenue
Springfield, MO 65804
800-443-1083
www.globaluniversity.edu
(*Christian Bible School)

Louisiana State University
Independent and Distance Learning
1225 Pleasant Hall
Baton Rouge, LA 70803

800-234-5046
www.lsu.edu

Ohio University
Life Long and Distance Learning
College Program for the Incarcerated (CPI)
Hanning Hall 222
Athens, OH 45701
800-444-2810
www.ohio.edu

GRADUATE CORRESPONDENCE DEGREE PROGRAMS

California Coast University
700 North Main Street
Santa Ana, CA 92701
888-228-8648
www.calcoast.edu

Global University School of Graduate Studies
1211 South Glenstone Avenue
Springfield, MO 65804
www.globaluniversity.edu
(*Christian bible College)

Northwestern California University
2151 River Plaza Drive Suite 306
Sacramento, CA 95833
916-920-9470
www.nwculaw.edu
(Juris Doctor (JD) Program/Law School)

BIBLE SCHOOL NON DEGREE PROGRAMS

American Bible Academy
P.O. Box 1627
Joplin, MO 64802

CrossRoad Bible Institute
P.O. Box 900
Grand Rapids, MI 49509

Rhema Correspondence Bible School
P.O. Box 50220
Tulsa, OK 74150

PARALEGAL STUDIES NON-DEGREE CERTIFICATION

Adams State College
208 Edgemont Boulevard
Alamosa, CO 81102
800-548-6679
www.adams.edu

Ashworth College
430 Technology Parkway
Norcross, GA 30092
800-640-9524
www.ashworth.edu

KEY TERMS AND DEFINITIONS

CORRESPONDENCE COURSES - Courses that can be taken through the mail that do not require Internet access. Correspondence courses vary from certificate programs to degree programs.

DISTANCE EDUCATION TRAINING COUNCIL (DETC) - An accreditation council recognized by Government, private work force and other civil service industries.

SENTRY CREDIT - Credit given to inmates for participation in certain Recreation and Education classes. These credits help to reduce the security levels of inmate participants.

Chapter 10
Prison Programs and Services

Knowing What The BOP Has To Offer

A great deal of the structure of Federal prison is built around the programs and services the BOP offers inmates. Not only does the BOP provide housing, their goal is to ensure inmates receive proper healthcare services and adequate programs to meet rehabilitation and re-entry needs. In this chapter, I will inform you of your rights and responsibilities regarding BOP programs and services. It is my hope you will utilize this information to make the best out of your term of incarceration.

HEALTH & MEDICAL SERVICES

While in the custody of the BOP "you have the right to receive health care in a manner that recognizes your basic human rights." Routine medical care is offered within each institution. Additionally, an inmate may be sent to local community medical facilities or transferred to a medical correctional facility for care beyond the scope of services offered within the institution.

Within 14 days of arrival, an inmate can expect to receive a physical examination that includes lab work, hearing and sight screening. The BOP will medically clear the inmate or give a synopsis of medical limitations and restrictions before placing them in a job assignment. Inmates that have severe medical conditions may be designated Medically Unassigned/Totally Disabled deeming them unemployable due to their physical or mental disability.

Truthfully, there may be times when you feel you are not being treated humanely and may feel you are not receiving proper medical attention. Medical care is generally marginal, but adequate in most cases. Do not expect services to include anything other than basic care. If you feel the care you are given is not sufficient, there is an inmate grievance process to follow for health care concerns. As with other concerns, you may submit your complaint in writing to the Medical staff in a Cop Out. If you do not obtain relief, you can follow the Administrative Remedy Process, which will be detailed in Chapter 11.

SICK CALL

Generally between the hours of 6:00 a.m. - 7:00 a.m., Monday through Friday, sick inmates may report to their designated medical office where a doctor, nurse or physicians' assistant will determine if medication or further treatment is needed. The inmate will be required to complete a sick call request form before being seen. After examination, if the medical staff confirms an inmate is sick, an 'Idle', which is a temporary disability excuse from work and activity, may be issued for up to three days. If the medical staff deems the inmate's sick call an emergency, a same day appointment will be scheduled. If not, the inmate will be issued an appointment for a later date. In this case, the inmate will be placed on the Call Out for the date of the appointment. If an inmate becomes ill outside of sick call hours, he or she should ask the work supervisor or CO to contact the Health Services on their behalf. Always be prepared to show identification for any health care visit.

DENTAL

All Federal institutions provide dental care to inmates. Dental care consists of teeth cleanings, fillings, tooth pulling and prosthesis care. Inmates are not eligible for accessory care such as orthodontic services, bridge or crown work.

Generally, all A&O inmates are seen by the Dental Department prior to being medically cleared. Inmates can request dental care by submitting a Cop Out to the Dental Department or by attending Dental sick call, which normally runs concurrent to Medical sick call times and procedures. All inmates may also take advantage of one dental cleaning per year and are eligible for routine dental care.

PREVENTATIVE HEALTH CARE

Preventative appointments are designed to review an inmate's health needs and provide preventative health care services. An inmate may refuse any part, or all parts, of a preventative examination. However, he or she must report to the Call Out appointment to avoid disciplinary action.

For female inmates, preventative services may include EKG, blood pressure screenings, blood work, PAP smear test and mammogram. Mammograms are offered every year at age 50 or older and every 3 years for inmates under age 50.

For male inmates preventative services may include EKG, blood pressure screenings, blood work and rectal examinations.

All inmates are scheduled for mandatory TB screenings and are offered the flu shot annually. Inmates meeting the CDC's guidelines for immunizations are given first priority for the influenza vaccine. All requests for flu shots should be made by submitting a Cop Out to your institution's Medical department.

PILL LINE & PHARMACY

Throughout the day inmate prescriptions are dispensed through the institution's Health Services Department. Restricted medications are issued on a dose-by-dose basis. Inmates are required to take the restricted medication in the presence of the pill line Medical staff. The medication may be crushed before dispensing and Medical staff may inspect the inmate's mouth after taking the medication to ensure it has been ingested.

If you are receiving restricted medications, you are required to report to pill line at the designated times each day. You may refuse the medication, but just like a Call Out, you must report to avoid disciplinary action. Pill line schedules will vary from institution to institution, but generally it is held for one hour, 2-3 times daily. Always be prepared to show identification to receive medications.

Non-restricted medications are dispensed through the Health Services Departments. If you take prescribed medications, you may pick them up daily at pill line. Medications are refilled through TRULINCS prior to the expiration date printed on the container. You should request refills at least 2 days prior to when it is needed. On TRULINCS click on the Prescription Refill button. You will then see a list of your prescribed medications. Only prescriptions due for refill will be listed. Click on the box to the left of the desired medication to send your refill request to Health Services. You may pick up your prescription usually within a day or two. Once a medication is expired, refilling it must be done through sick call.

Over the counter (OTC) items such as Ibuprofen, eye drops, multi-vitamins and allergy pills may be purchased on Commissary on your designated shopping day. (See Commissary List at the end of Chapter 7). It is best to plan ahead and have OTC items available for use when the Commissary is closed. OTC items do not count toward your Commissary spending limit, so stock up because Health Services will not issue items for treatment that are available on Commissary.

PSYCHOLOGY & MENTAL HEALTH SERVICES

All BOP facilities offer mental health services through the Psychology Services Department. An inmate can expect to meet with a member of the Psychology staff within the first few weeks of their incarceration. The purpose of the initial visit is to review the inmate's history, identify their psychological needs, review the BOP policy as it relates to their department and review how to seek out services when needed. This is also the time to ask about programs like drug abuse treatment or mental health counseling.

To contact a Psychology staff member, inmates may submit a Cop Out or Inmate Request, locate a Psychology staff member during mainline or notify any staff member in a crisis situation.

It is common for inmates to experience depression while in prison. However, over time most inmates adapt to their incarceration. If you or another inmate are struggling to cope with your incarceration, you should contact a staff member immediately to seek psychological services. If you are contemplating suicide or are in danger of hurting yourself or others, talk to a staff member immediately. It is also the responsibility of each inmate to seek out Psychology Services if they suspect another inmate is contemplating suicide.

RESOLVE PROGRAM

Many federal institutions offer a non-residential program called Resolve for inmates who have a history of physical or sexual abuse. The psycho-educational part of this program is the Trauma in Life Workshop for inmates dealing with challenges related to traumatic life events. This component gives the inmate coping strategies following traumatic life events. Non-residential counseling groups are also a vital part of the Resolve program. These groups help inmates improve coping skills, build relationships and improve emotional stability.

SPECIALIZED MENTAL HEALTH PROGRAMS

The BOP has many residential mental health programs for inmates with severe emotional, cognitive and behavioral problems. The goal of these programs is to help inmates improve their day to day functioning and prevent a need for hospitalization.

SKILLS PROGRAM

The Skills program is a residential treatment program to help inmates with intellectual and emotional difficulties adjust to institutional living. An inmate will likely be identified at intake if they are a candidate for the Skills program.

SEX OFFENDER MANAGEMENT PROGRAM (SOMP)

The BOP offers Sex Offender Management programs at certain Federal facilities where a higher proportion of sex offenders compose their general population. This is to ensure that inmates in treatment feel safe about participating in the program.

There are two levels of treatment offered: 1) The Residential Sex Offender Treatment Program (SOTP-R) for high risk offenders such as inmates with multiple offenses. (Currently this program is facilitated at the FMC in Devens, Massachusetts). 2) The Non-Residential Sex Offender Treatment Program (SOTP-NR) is a moderately intensive program designed for lower risk offenders such as first time offenders. (This program is facilitated at all SOMP institutions).

Treatment programs are voluntary and an inmate can apply at any time during their incarceration by submitting a Cop Out to Psychology Services. If eligible, an inmate is accepted and transferred to a SOMP institution. Inmates ordinarily enter SOMP programs if they have 24 to 42 months remaining on their sentence.

DRUG ABUSE EDUCATION COURSE (DAEC)

The Drug Abuse Education course is offered at all BOP facilities. It is NOT drug treatment. It is a program that gives inmates the chance to review the consequences of their drug use, how their drug use may be related to their crime and provides an opportunity for inmates to view how their lives might be without being under the influence of drugs. The ultimate goal of the program is to encourage inmates to request drug treatment. Inmates are required to attend DAEC if their PSR shows a history of drug use, evidence that drugs or alcohol contributed to the commission of the crime, the Judge recommends treatment or a violation of community supervision has occurred. Should an inmate decline enrollment in the DAEC when it is mandated on their PSR, they will become ineligible to receive performance pay above maintenance pay level, which is currently $5.25 per month. Additionally, inmates who decline participation will become ineligible for vacation or bonus pay. Inmates may volunteer for the DAEC program, even if they are not mandated, by submitting a Cop Out or Inmate Request to Staff to Psychology Services.

NON-RESIDENTIAL DRUG ABUSE TREATMENT

"Non-Res" Drug Abuse treatment is available at all BOP facilities. The program is geared toward inmates with a minor drug abuse problem and inmates who are eligible but do not have sufficient time to complete the more intense Residential Drug Abuse Program (RDAP). Additionally, inmates who are awaiting placement in an RDAP program and inmates who have an interest in staying sober in their community upon release may attend the program.

RESIDENTIAL DRUG ABUSE TREATMENT (RDAP)

The Residential Drug Abuse Treatment Program (RDAP) provides intensive drug abuse treatment for inmates diagnosed with a drug abuse treatment or drug use disorder. Through a group based, nine month program, inmates are housed together in a modified therapeutic community which is separated from the general population. The RDAP is a half-day program, with the rest of the day devoted to work, school, and other self-improvement activities. Participants are required to model the pro-social behaviors expected in a community, demonstrating honesty, positive peer relations and group participation.

Inmates who are diagnosed with a drug use disorder are qualified for RDAP and are admitted based on their projected release date. Eligible inmates must have enough time left on their sentence to complete the entire program, which includes follow-up treatment in a Residential Re-entry Center (RRC) or on home confinement.

Upon successful completion of RDAP, participants are eligible to receive up to a year off of their term of imprisonment in accordance with the Violent Crime Control and Law Enforcement Act of 1994. This act stipulates that if the felony committed by a participant involves physical force, threats, possession or use of a firearm or other dangerous weapons, or sexual abuse committed upon minors, he or she will be ineligible to receive an early release for program completion.

Currently RDAP is available in 62 institutions. Inmates who are interested in participating may submit a Cop Out or Inmate Request to the Drug Abuse Program Coordinator. The Coordinator will conduct an interview to determine if the applicant qualifies. Generally, inmates are interviewed between 42 - 24 months from release depending on the facility's security level and waiting list for RDAP.

RELIGIOUS SERVICES

Federal regulations and BOP policy provides for pastoral care and practice of individual and group religious beliefs. Chaplains offer religious support, education and counseling to meet inmates' diverse religious needs. The Chaplain is also responsible for the religious diet program, ceremonial religious meals and religious holiday observances.

Inmates may possess religious property subject to safety and security regulations and verified of its religious significance through the Chaplain or Warden. Some items of religious property may include, medallions, hijabs, rosary beads, oils, rugs and medicine pouches. All religious property must be purchased through the Commissary or Special Purchase Order (SPO) and cannot be valued over $100. (For more information on religious items permitted in Federal prison see BOP Program Statement P5360.09).

THRESHOLD PROGRAM

The Threshold Program is a six month, spirituality based program offered through Chaplaincy Services. The program is designed to help inmates address major life issues and promote understanding and growth. There are three phases to the program - Orientation, Personal Growth & Development and Relationships. Inmates who successfully complete the entire program are invited to participate in a graduation ceremony attended by staff and fellow inmates. In some institutions, family members may even be invited to attend. Program participants receive Sentry credit for rehabilitative programming, which help reduce the inmate's security level and chances of recidivism. To participate in this program, an inmate should submit a Cop Out to Chaplaincy Services.

EDUCATION

Education is a key component of rehabilitative services offered by the BOP. Institutions are required by law to provide mandatory literacy and English as a Second Language (ESL). Additionally, the Education Department is required to provide education/recreation related programs that meet the needs and interests of the inmate population, provide options for the positive use of inmate time and to enhance successful reintegration into the community.

As a new inmate, expect to be scheduled to meet with someone from the Education Department within the first week of your arrival. This appointment will be set to determine your educational level and your participation in educational and recreational programs in the past. Generally, prior to sentencing, the U.S. Probation Department will verify your educational history. This process is done by checking your high school and college transcripts. If this was done, the verified information will be included in your PSR. If not, you will be required to show proof you have either a high school diploma or General Equivalency Diploma (GED). If you do not have either of these credentials, you will be required to attend GED Education classes while incarcerated.

I have witnessed college graduates who had to enroll in the GED program because they did not have the required proof of their high school diploma. To avoid this fate, make sure your high school diploma is verified in your PSR. If not, make a copy of the documentation and have it held by someone who can mail it directly to an Education Staff member to verify your completion.

LITERACY/GED

The Violent Crime Control and Law Enforcement Act (VCCLEA) and the Prison Litigation Act (PLRA) requires inmates who lack a high school diploma to participate in a GED credential program. The enforcement of inmates participation is to receive their good time credit and job pay promotions, an inmate must earn a GED or participate in GED instruction for a mandatory 240 hours. Inmates who complete the mandatory period of enrollment and have not earned their diploma, must re-enroll in order to receive their good conduct time.

Inmates who receive an incident report related to their literacy program enrollment will be labeled GED UNSATISFACTORY PROGRESS and will not be awarded good conduct time. In addition, they will be required to complete an additional 240 classroom hours before obtaining SATISFACTORY status.

ENGLISH AS A SECOND LANGUAGE (ESL)

Non-English speaking Federal inmates must participate in an ESL program and will be referred to the Education Department upon arrival for testing. Inmates scoring below 8th grade level in proficiency will be placed in an ESL program until they eventually function at the required level. Even if a non-English speaking inmate has a high school diploma or a college degree, he or she will still be required to participate in ESL classes.

APPRENTICESHIPS

Apprenticeship programs in the BOP are sponsored by the U.S. Department of Labor and provide on-the-job training in specialized fields to prepare inmates for future employment. Programs range from 2,000 - 8,000 hours in length or approximately 2,000 hours per year. Successful inmates will earn a Certificate of Completion from the Department of Labor and may use that certificate to enter a career field upon release. Prior credit hours may be awarded to inmates at inception to the program. Programs vary from institution to institution but may include:

Administrative Assistant	4,000 hours
Animal Trainer	4,000 hours
Baker	6,000 hours
Carpenter	8,000 hours
Chaplain Support Service	2,000 hours
Cook	6,000 hours
Dental Assistant	2,000 hours

Education and Training	2,500 hours
Electrician	8,000 hours
Housekeeper	2,000 hours
Landscape Management Technician	2,000 hours
Legal Secretary	2,000 hours
Material Coordinator	4,000 hours
Meat Cutter	4,000 hours
Painter	6,000 hours
Plumber	8,000 hours
Quality Control Inspector	4,000 hours
Recreation Assistant	4,500 hours
Stationary Engineer	8,000 hours
Teacher's Aide	4,000 hours
Tool Machine Set Up Operator	6,000 hours
Undercar Specialist	4,000 hours

ADULT CONTINUING EDUCATION (ACE)

ACE programs at BOP facilities are available to inmates who are interested in expanding their knowledge or learning new skills. These classes are generally taught by other inmates who have specialized knowledge in a particular field. Courses range in length from 6 - 16 weeks. BOP Staff members and outside volunteer instructors may also instruct ACE classes.

Inmates are notified of ACE course offerings through the TRULINCS Bulletin Board and flyers are generally posted in housing units. Participants are chosen by lottery or on a first come first served basis. With the exception given to classes such as Lifeskills, Parenting and Job Readiness, an inmate may only enroll in one ACE class at a time.

If an inmate chooses to drop a class for any reason or does not follow class rules, they risk being placed on the ACE Drop List, disallowing enrollment in any other ACE course for a six month probationary period.

Parenting, Foreign Languages, Business classes, Computer Applications and Medical Terminology are offered as ACE courses, along with a variety of other classes, which will vary at different institutions. ACE classes can be very rewarding as they give inmates an opportunity to explore a variety of different topics in a unique setting. Many skills learned through the classes will be helpful for re-entry.

CAREER RESOURCE CENTER (CRC)

The CRC at every Federal institution aims to help inmates meet career goals and prepare for a successful re-entry into their community. Inmate Career Technicians provide resume and portfolio preparation assistance, share potential employment information, inform inmates of available community resources and social services for re-entry, administer career interest exams and provide educational and training resources. The CRC also assists inmates with information on correspondence courses.

MOTHERS & INFANTS NURTURING TOGETHER (MINT)

The MINT program is available to women who are pregnant and incarcerated in the Federal prison system. The program is designed to promote bonding between a mother and her newborn and to enhance parenting skills. If a woman is pregnant at sentencing, she may self-surrender or be remanded directly to a MINT facility. However, this individual must ask to be enrolled in the program. It will not be offered without inquiry. Once designated to a facility, referral to the MINT program may also be made by the Unit Team, including the Case Manager.

RRC MINT PROGRAM

Most MINT programs are operated through a Residential Re-entry Center (RRC) contracted with the BOP and mothers are allowed to stay there with their infant for 3-6 months. Expectant mothers give birth at the local hospital nearest to the RRC and are afforded time to be with their newborn child. After completion of the program, the inmate is sent back to the Federal facility they have been designated to in order to complete their sentence and their child is sent to live with a family member or friend of the inmate's choice. If an inmate is nearing the end of their sentence, mother and child may be allowed to remain at the RRC as part of their normal re-entry process.

Inmates who participate in the MINT program are expected to provide financially for themselves and their child. If an inmate is suffering from financial hardship, she may seek the assistance of Social Services.

RESIDENTIAL MINT PROGRAM

A longer term MINT program is offered at one facility: The GreenBrier Birthing Center in Hillsboro, West Virginia. Independently contracted through the BOP, the GreenBrier is operated similar to other re-entry center MINT programs, except an inmate may stay up to 12 months in the program in order to bond with their child.

Although the inmate is responsible for supporting themselves financially, the child is placed on Medicaid, WIC and food stamps. As in all federal facilities, the inmate's spending limit is $320.00 per month but many items such as diapers and toiletries are donated through community groups. Pre-approved well child visits are performed at local physician's offices at the expense of the BOP.

To be eligible for this program, the inmate must be Camp status, have committed a non-violent offense and have 5 years or less remaining on their sentence. For placement assistance in an appropriate MINT program, inmates may contact Prison Consulting Group in Largo, FL at 800-382-0868 or prisoncgroup@yahoo.com

CONCLUSION

Keep in mind the programs and services each institution offers may vary. Therefore, inquire about the programs your institution has to offer and refer to your institution's A&O manual for further details. Stay informed and utilize the resources offered to you. Participating in BOP services and programs will help you sustain a healthy morale while preparing you to embrace your successful future.

CHAPTER 10: KNOWING WHAT THE BOP HAS TO OFFER

KEY TERMS AND DEFINITIONS

ADULT CONTINUING EDUCATION (ACE) - Educational classes offered at most BOP institutions often taught by inmates. Sentry credit is awarded upon successful completion of an ACE class.

APPRENTICESHIP - A program sponsored by the U.S. Department of Labor providing inmates with on-the-job training and education in specialized fields.

DRUG ABUSE EDUCATION COURSE (DAEC) - A mandatory program offered at all BOP facilities for inmates who have a history of drug use.

ELECTROCARDIOGRAM (EKG) - A screening administered to new inmates and annually to other inmates, which assesses the condition of the heart.

ENGLISH AS A SECOND LANGUAGE (ESL) - A mandatory program for non-English speaking inmates scoring below an 8th grade level in English proficiency.

GENERAL EQUIVALENCY DIPLOMA (GED) - A mandatory credential program for inmates who have not earned a high school diploma.

IDLE - A written disability excuse, issued through the Health Services Department, from work and other activities for up to 3 days of absence.

MOTHERS INFANTS NURTURING TOGETHER (MINT) PROGRAM - A 3-6 month program available to women who are pregnant and incarcerated in the Federal prison system. Non-residential MINT programs are operated through RRCs. The 12 month, residential MINT program is offered at one BOP facility in West Virginia.

OTC MEDICATIONS - Over the Counter, non-prescription medications such as ibuprofen, eye drops, and allergy medicines available for purchase from Commissary.

PILL LINE - The daily issuance of restricted medications by a Medical Staff officer where inmates form a line for individual, supervised distribution.

RESIDENTIAL DRUG ABUSE TREATMENT PROGRAM (RDAP) - An intensive drug abuse treatment offered to inmates who have been diagnosed with a drug abuse disorder. Participation in this 500-hour course can grant inmates up to 12 months off their sentence.

RESIDENTIAL RE-ENTRY CENTER (RRC) - (See Halfway House) A community transitional home, operated under the BOP, where inmates spend up to a year from their release transitioning back into society.

RESOLVE PROGRAM - A BOP non-residential program offered to inmates who have a history of physical or sexual abuse.

SEX OFFENDER MANAGEMENT PROGRAM (SOMP) - A voluntary sex offender program offered at certain federal facilities.

SPECIAL PURCHASE ORDER (SPO) - Special orders placed by inmates for items not available on Commissary such as craft items and religious articles.

WOMEN, INFANTS, CHILDREN (WIC) - A program offering dairy products and other groceries free of charge to women, infants and children in need.

Chapter 11

Legal Remedies From Behind Bars

Justice for Inmates!

By: Jamila T. Davis

When I came through the doors of Federal prison, I was faced with many additional legal challenges. I had already been sentenced to 12 1/2 years for bank fraud in New Jersey, yet still had another federal case in Santa Ana, California, a separate federal probation violation and a pending state case in New Jersey. Overwhelmed is an understatement of the feelings that flooded my mind at the time.

Aside from praying, I had done very little else in my own defense, having trusted my attorney who assured me that everything was under control. I assumed he had it all covered, but I was wrong. It wasn't until I hit the compound and entered the law library that I discovered how little my attorney actually knew about Federal white collar law.

For many hours, from sun up to sun down, I studied law books. I read the commentary of the U.S. Sentencing Guidelines over and over again and studied the Federal Rule Book. I was amazed at how much I learned in such a short period of time.

By the time my attorney came to visit me, I was armed with a book full of notes. He was advising me to take a plea agreement in the Santa Ana case that would run concurrent to my New Jersey case, but would cause me to owe an additional $1.2 million in restitution. I passed him the notes I jotted down about loss amount calculations and refused the offer. At the time, he thought I was absolutely insane, but I was willing to take my chances.

A few weeks later, my attorney came back to see me. He was astonished that the information I gave him was correct. Citing the Sentencing Guidelines Commentary, we were successful in lowering the loss amount to less than

CHAPTER 11: JUSTICE FOR INMATES!

$200,000, which also reduced the sentence substantially. Then I agreed to take the revised plea agreement.

Armed with the law, I was able to get my probation violation dismissed and my pending charge in New Jersey down to a minor offense. Had I known what I know today about the law, I would not be serving such a lengthy prison sentence. The most valuable lesson I learned was the power of knowing the law for myself.

During my 6 1/2 years of incarceration, I have won several legal battles for myself and for others with whom I was housed, which has made me a well sought after "Jail House" lawyer. Not only have I successfully filed motions in the U.S. Courts, I have also had victories challenging BOP policy violations. As I discussed previously in this book, it is my goal to further my knowledge by attending law school, via correspondence courses, from behind bars. My experience has given me the faith to realize I can help many others balance the scales of justice.

In this chapter, it is my goal to share with you the basics of what I've learned concerning the BOP legal remedy process, and provide helpful tips for gaining post conviction relief. If you are experiencing legal difficulties or feel you have been treated unjustly, I urge you to use your time during incarceration to study the law. It is not as difficult as you may think to gain relief!

UTILIZING THE LAW LIBRARY COMPUTER

It is vital you familiarize yourself with the Law Library in your institution. There is pertinent information you can obtain and people you will meet in your institution who can help you.

One of the most valuable resources we have, as inmates, is access to the Law Library computers through TRULINCS. This data base is filled with useful publications including the BOP Program Statement, U.S. Code Service, U.S. Sentencing Guidelines, U.S. Constitution, Federal Court Rules, Code of Federal Regulations, Supreme Court Reports, Shepard's Federal Citations, BNA Criminal Law Reporter, Bender's Federal Practice Forms, Constitutional Rights of Prisoners, Federal

Habeus Corpus Practice and Procedure, The Law Dictionary, Prisoner's Assistance Directory, Court Addresses, Criminal Law Deskbook, Legal Research Guide, Moore's Federal and Practice - Criminal. Through Lexis Nexis on the Law Library system, you can also access all U.S. District Courts and Courts of Appeals, including the District of Columbia, in the United States.

The Law Library computer is an invaluable tool that can substantially help inmates. To familiarize yourself with using the library, when you log on to the computer, scroll down to the option: Lexis Nexis Electronic Law Library Training Manual. The training manual is simple to read and will quickly inform you how to perform your research. Utilizing simple search options allows you to look up anything you want to know using key terms.

BOP PROGRAM POLICY STATEMENT

The BOP is governed in accordance with the BOP Program Policy Statement, which is a set of standard rules and procedures for all internal operations. Just as the Federal courts abide by Federal law, the BOP abides by it's program statement. If you are accused of breaking BOP policy, as an inmate, you have the right to challenge the action. This can be done through the BOP legal remedy process.

In order to know if policy has been violated, you have to know what the policy states. It is my suggestion that you start with reading your institution's A&O manual, which you will be given shortly after arrival. Additionally, you can pull up the BOP Program Statement utilizing the Law Library computers through TRULINCS. It is a good idea to browse through the entire policy to familiarize yourself with its contents.

BOP LEGAL REMEDY PROCESS

The first step in addressing an institutional issue at your facility is to submit a Cop Out or BP-8.5 addressed to the direct staff member or department where the issue exists. If you do not get an acceptable response, you may then begin the legal remedy process.

Just like the U.S. Courts, the BOP is a bureaucracy that strictly follows the chain of command. Therefore, certain steps must be taken in order for your issue to be properly addressed. If you miss any of these steps, your matter may be dismissed.

The BOP legal remedy process officially starts by requesting a BP-9 from your Counselor. This form can only be requested after you have completed the informal resolution process, which is your attempt to handle the matter directly with the staff member or department where the issue arose. The BP-9 is a formal written Administrative Remedy Request that is submitted directly to the Warden of the institution for response. A BP-9 must be submitted within 20 calendar days following the date the issue in question occurred.

This form must be carefully completed documenting, in detail, the problem and the violation of BOP policy if known. This document can be typed or hand written. If handwritten, make sure your words are legible. If there is not enough room on the BP-9 form to complete your statement, you may use one letter-size (8 1/2" x 11") page. Be sure to make a copy of this extra page to submit with your filing.

The Warden has up to 20 calendar days to respond to your BP-9. If you are not satisfied with the Warden's answer, you may appeal by submitting a BP-10 to the Regional office within 20 calendar days of receiving the Warden's response.

Just like the BP-9, a BP-10 can be obtained from your Counselor. The BP-10 must be completely filled out with all requested identifying information and the reasons for the appeal stated in the space provided. If more space is needed, you may use one letter-size (8 1/2" x 11") continuation page. If you utilize an extra page you MUST submit two additional copies of that page and two copies of any exhibits you may have enclosed. Your exhibits will include your BP-9 denial from the Warden. This is very important! If you do not have the correct amount of copies enclosed, your filing may be rejected!

Once your BP-10 is filed, the Regional Director has 20 calendar days to respond. If you are not satisfied with the response the Director renders, you can appeal the decision by submitting a BP-11.

Once again, the BP-11 form can be obtained from your Counselor. It must be submitted to the BOP General Counsel within 30 calendar days from the date of the Regional Director's response. This filing may also contain up to one continuation page on a letter-size (8 1/2" x 11") page. If you have a continuation page, you must submit three copies along with three copies of all exhibits, which will include your previous BP-9 and BP-10 responses.

The Central Office will have up to 30 calendar days to answer your BP-11. If you are not satisfied with the response, then you can start a law suit by filing a 2241 Motion with the District Court where your institution is located in accordance with 28 U.S.C.S 2241. To gain more information on how to file a 2241 law suit, I recommend that you purchase "A Prisoner's Survival Guide" by John Belanger. This book will guide you step-by-step through the process.

INMATE DISCIPLINARY PROCEDURES

When a BOP staff member witnesses or reasonably believes an inmate has committed a prohibited act, he or she may issue an incident report, which is a written copy of the charges against an inmate. Within 24 hours of the time staff became aware of the incident, the incident report must be delivered to the inmate directly.

Once an incident report is issued, the matter can either be resolved through informal resolution or it may be referred to the Disciplinary Hearing Officer (DHO). If an informal resolution is provided by the Unit Disciplinary Committee (UDC), the incident report will be removed from the inmate's central file. An informal resolution may include a warning or punishment such as extra duty. Informal resolutions are encouraged for all violations in the Moderate and Low severity categories. Disciplinary proceedings may be suspended for up to two calendar weeks while an informal resolution is undertaken. All violations in the Greatest and High severity categories must be forwarded to the DHO for final disposition.

Inmates will be given an initial hearing within five working days from the day the incident report is issued, excluding the day it was issued, as well as weekends and holidays. The Warden must approve, in writing, any extension over five days. The initial hearing is held before the UDC. The charged inmate is entitled to be present for the hearing, and he or she may make statements and present documentary evidence. The decision from the UDC must be given in writing by the close of the next work day after the hearing. The UDC may make findings on Moderate and Low severity offenses, but will automatically refer Greatest and High severity offenses to the DHO for final disposition. The UDC may also make recommendations for punishment to the DHO.

DISCIPLINE HEARING OFFICER (DHO)

The DHO is employed by the BOP. He or she makes routine visits to different institutions to preside over disciplinary hearings, on all Greatest and High severity prohibited acts and other violations referred by the Unit Disciplinary Committee (UDC). The DHO will only hear cases referred by the UDC.

All inmates accused of violations must receive a copy of their written charges no less than 24 hours before seeing the DHO. Appearances for the DHO hearing may be made in person or through video or telephone conference. An inmate has the right to make statements and present documentary evidence. He or she may also request that witnesses appear to provide testimony.

The DHO will call witnesses who have information directly relevant to the charge(s) and who are reasonably available. Those witnesses who are not available will be requested to provide a statement to the DHO.

During the hearing, inmates are not allowed to directly question witnesses. Instead, inmates will be assigned a staff member representative who can ask questions on behalf of the inmate. In the case that a staff member is unavailable, the charged inmate may present a list of questions for the witnesses which the DHO officer can ask directly.

After the hearing, a written copy of the decision and disposition is ordinarily given within 15 days of the decision.

APPEALS OF DISCIPLINARY ACTIONS

Appeals of all disciplinary actions may be made through the Administrative Remedy process, which was detailed earlier in this chapter. The UDC's decision can be appealed directly to the Warden of the institution. Decisions of the DHO are final and subject to review only by the Regional Director. Therefore, you would need to go to your Counselor and request a BP-230 to be sent to the Regional Director to appeal a DHO ruling. If you are unhappy with the response, you can then request a BP-231 to be sent to Central Office/General Counsel, following the Administrative Remedy process.

On appeal, the reviewing authority (Warden, Regional Director or General Counsel) considers:

1. Whether the UDC or DHO substantially complied with regulations on inmate discipline.
2. Whether the UDC or DHO based its decision on facts. If there is conflicting evidence, whether the decision was based on the greater weight of the evidence.
3. Whether an appropriate sanction was imposed for the severity level of the prohibited act, and other relevant circumstances.

It is my suggestion that when challenging any claim, you do your homework. Spend time on the Law Library computer and research the BOP Disciplinary Procedures and the Administrative Remedy process in the Program Statement. Know the rules and procedures so you can effectively defend yourself!

HOW TO HANDLE OUTSTANDING DETAINERS

As an inmate, if you are looking to obtain Halfway House placement, you can not have any outstanding detainers. A detainer is a hold on an inmate for unresolved warrants or pending charges. Additionally, detainers may increase your security level and jeopardize lower level housing. Therefore, it is my suggestion that you try your best to get rid of all pending charges.

CHAPTER 11: JUSTICE FOR INMATES!

As I explained earlier in this chapter, I had several pending charges when I was first incarcerated. Consequently, I was designated to an FCI. While spending time in the Law Library, I learned about the Interstate Agreement Detainer Act (IADA). It is a contract between forty-eight states, (excluding Mississippi and Louisiana) the Federal government and the District of Columbia. (See 18 U.S.C.S App. 2). The agreement "provides for expeditious delivery of the prisoner to the receiving State for trial prior to the termination of his sentence in the sending State." (Alabama v. Bozeman, 533 U.S. 146, 148, 121S. Ct. 2079, 150 L. Ed. 2d 188 (2001).

Once a detainer is lodged against an inmate, he or she may submit a motion to the Court, in accordance with IADA (See 18 U.S.C.S App. 2) requesting that the matter is handled expeditiously. In that case, the state or government has 120 days from the time that the IADA is filed to be brought to trial on the matter. If not, the case must be dismissed.

This act was established to ensure the defendant is given a speedy trial, and to minimize interruption of the defendant's on-going rehabilitation or prison treatment program. I found the IADA to be quite useful because it required the state to act immediately and resolve my pending issues. From the date I lodged my IADA, I was shipped out to handle the charges within two weeks. Once I resolved the matter, I was no longer FCI status. Therefore, I was sent to a Camp.

You can file an IADA motion on your own by seeking help in the Law Library. Or, you can make a formal request through the records office of your institution. In my case, I had the Warden sign my IADA which was sent to the Court. In any case, make sure you send out your motion through legal mail. According to the Mailbox Rule, your motion is filed with the Courts the date that a prison official logs your mail in the legal mail record book. Therefore, make sure you have proof that it was officially logged and deemed filed. Then start counting the days! After 120 days, if you haven't been taken to trial, your case must be dismissed.

WAYS TO GAIN RELIEF FROM THE COURTS

It's easy to get into prison, but difficult to get out! After you have been sentenced to serve time, there are only a few ways to have your conviction overturned or your sentence reduced, which we will discuss in this section.

1. Direct Appeal - Within 14 days after you are sentenced, your attorney can file a notice of appeal to your sentencing Court. Upon receipt of this notice, the direct appeal process will begin. All offenders are entitled to receive attorney representation on direct appeal. If you win your direct appeal, your conviction can be overturned, thrown out, or your case can be remanded for resentencing.

2. 2255 Motion - A prisoner in custody may file a 2255 Motion, in accordance with 28 U.S.C.S 2255, to the Court which imposed the sentence, seeking to vacate, set aside or correct the sentence on the following grounds: 1) his or her sentence was imposed in violation of the Constitution or laws of the United States, 2) the court was without jurisdiction to impose such sentence, 3) the sentence was in excess of the maximum authorized by law, or 4) the sentence is otherwise subject to collateral attack.

    2255 Motions are commonly submitted for ineffective counsel. Under the Strickland Supreme Court rule, if you can show that your attorney made an error that prejudiced your case and caused you to receive a higher sentence, you may have a valid Strickland claim that can help you gain relief.

    You can only file a 2255 Motion within a year of your conviction or within 15 months of the denial of your direct appeal. This motion can only be filed once, so make sure you include all valid claims. You may hire an attorney to file this motion for you, or you may choose to do it pro se. If you are considering filing pro se, I highly recommend that you purchase the book "A Prisoner's Guide to Survival" by John Belanger. He details the process for filing and provides very good case law.

3. Rule 35 Motion - The Government, at any time within a year of your conviction, can file a Rule 35 Motion and have you brought back to testify or cooperate with them in the prosecution of someone else. If this occurs, you will be eligible for a sentence reduction.
4. 3582 Motion - If a defendant has been sentenced to a term of imprisonment based on a sentencing range that has subsequently been lowered by the Sentencing Commission pursuant to 28 U.S.C.S 994 (o), a 3582 Motion can be submitted to the courts in accordance with 18 U.S.C.S 3582 requesting a time reduction based on the new guidelines.

Since my incarceration, I witnessed numerous inmates receive reductions in their sentences based on the new Drug Laws. The BOP is substantially overcrowded. New remedies are in the works including relief for White Collar defendants!

HOW TO FILE A MOTION TO REDUCE FRP PAYMENTS

As discussed earlier, all inmates who have fines or restitution are required to participate in the FRP program. Unless your judge has issued a Court order for you to pay the minimum amount of $25.00 each quarter, you will be subject to pay up to 50% of the gross funds received in your Commissary account. For many, this amount can be several hundred dollars a month.

Watching a fellow inmate whom I was housed with experience financial difficulties trying to keep up on her imposed FRP payment, I researched and helped her submit a motion which we won to reduce her payment while incarcerated.

We submitted a Motion to Modify the Restitution Order pursuant to 18 U.S.C.S 3664(k). According to this statute, if the defendant has any material change in "economic circumstances that might affect the defendant's ability to pay restitution . . . the Court may adjust the payment schedule."

In the Motion, we provided documentation of her finances, showing the change in her economic circumstances and the stress that the FRP payment caused her. The Judge granted her request and payments were reduced to $25.00 per quarter until she was released from prison. (See U.S. v. Woolf-Turk, 2011 U.S. Dist. Lexis 91887, Southern District of New York).

You can also submit a Motion to Modify the Restitution Order to your Judge. It is my advice that you only provide truthful information in your motion. The U.S. Government WILL verify your claims and challenge them. You can look up the case as listed above on the Law Library Computer by pulling up the 2nd Circuit District Court and doing a search under the name Woolf-Turk. The Motion was granted August 16, 2011 by the Honorable Noemie Buchwald in the Southern District of New York.

CONCLUSION

My advice to all inmates is to continue to fight the good fight of faith. Never give up, especially if you feel you have been done wrong! Educate yourself to the law. You are your best advocate! Therefore, learn to defend yourself and stay out of trouble!

KEY TERMS AND DEFINITIONS

- **2241 MOTION** - A Motion in accordance with 28 U.S.C.S 2241 that prisoners can utilize to challenge: (1) an improper revocation of probation, (2) the computation of a sentence, (3) the revocation of sentencing credits, (4) how a sentence is being imposed, or (5) challenge the denial of bail.
- **2255 MOTION** - A Motion in accordance with 28 U.S.C.S 2255 seeking to vacate, set aside or correct the sentence of a prisoner filed within 12 months from the time he or she was sentenced, or 15 months from the denial of his or her direct appeal.
- **3582 MOTION** - A Motion to the Courts to reduce a prisoner's sentence based on new sentencing guideline ranges imposed by the Sentencing Commission, in accordance with 18 U.S.C.S 3582
- **BOP PROGRAM POLICY STATEMENT** - The set rules and procedures that govern the operations of the BOP.

BP-8.5 - The first step in the informal resolution process where an inmate lodges a complaint to the direct staff member or department where the problem occurred.

BP-9 - The first step in the Administrative Remedy process where an inmate appeals the decision of staff to the Warden.

BP-10 - The second step in the Administrative Remedy process where an inmate appeals the decision of the Warden to the Regional Director.

BP-11 - The third step in the Administrative Remedy process where an inmate appeals the Regional Director's decision to the Central Office/General Counsel.

BP-230 - The appeal request form used to challenge a DHO ruling, which goes to the BOP Regional Director.

BP-231 - The appeal request form used to challenge the BOP Regional Director's response regarding a DHO ruling, which goes to the Central Office/General Counsel.

DETAINER - A hold on an inmate for unresolved warrants or pending charges.

DIRECT APPEAL - An Appeal of the District Court's ruling to the Court of Appeals.

DISCIPLINARY HEARING OFFICER (DHO) - An officer who presides over disciplinary hearings on all Greatest and High severity prohibited acts and other violations referred by the Unit Disciplinary Committee (UDC).

INTERSTATE AGREEMENT DETAINER ACT (IADA) - A contract between forty-eight states (excluding Mississippi and Louisiana), the Federal Government and the District of Columbia, where an inmate must expeditiously be sent to face trial on a pending matter upon his or her demand, prior to the termination of their sentence in another state or jurisdiction.

MAILBOX RULE - The Federal Court rule that deems legal mail filed by inmates when it is handed to and logged in by a prison staff member.

PRO SE - The act of an inmate filing a motion without the assistance of an attorney. The inmate may NOT have an attorney of record.

RULE 35 MOTION - A motion from the Government, after sentencing, seeking to reduce a defendants' sentence for his or her cooperation with the Government.

UNIT DISCIPLINARY COMMITTEE (UDC) - A committee of Unit Team members who preside over disciplinary hearings and make findings on Moderate and Low severity level offenses.

U.S. SENTENCING GUIDELINES - Guidelines set by the U.S. Sentencing Commission that help Judges determine the sentencing range for offenders based on their offense.

Chapter 12
Federal Prison From A Woman's Perspective

Female Offenders Questions & Answers (Q&A)

When I entered the Danbury Federal Prison Camp in March 2014, the FCI was undergoing a 'mission' change. Over 1100 women were shipped to other facilities and the institution was being renovated to house men who would arrive shortly thereafter. In the media, there was great talk about how the families of these women would suffer, having to travel several hundred miles to visit. Unfortunately, being housed far away from home is a consequence for many women who are incarcerated in federal prisons. Even a recommendation from the Judge requesting placement in a facility close to home does not guarantee placement close to home. Hence, there are few facilities to house 14,000 female offenders. If the facility closest to your home is at capacity or if you have a cooperating co-conspirator designated to the same facility, chances are you will be housed in a facility far from home.

This chapter was written to give you some basic facts about the female facilities in the BOP and various perspectives on the programs, services and the structures of each of these facilities.

The BOP has 18 facilities that house sentenced female offenders. These facilities include 12 Camps:

Alderson FPC - Alderson, West Virginia
Aliceville FPC - Aliceville, Alabama
Bryan FPC - Bryan, Texas
Carswell FPC - Carswell, Texas
Coleman FPC - Coleman, Florida
Danbury FPC - Danbury, Connecticut
Dublin FPC - Dublin, California

Greenville FPC - Greenville, Illinois
Lexington FPC - Lexington, Kentucky
Marianna FPC - Marianna, Florida
Phoenix FPC - Phoenix, Arizona
Victorville FPC - Victorville, California

Additionally, there are five FCI facilities that house women:
Aliceville FCI - Aliceville, Alabama
Carswelll FMC - Carswell, Texas
Dublin FCI - Dublin, California
Tallahassee FCI - Tallahassee, Florida
Waseca FCI - Waseca, Minnesota

There is one high security facility for women offenders which is a United States Penitentiary (USP):
Hazleton USP - Hazleton, West Virginia

If you are a female sentenced to serve time, your prison sentence will be served in one of the above institutions.

While spending time at Danbury Federal Prison Camp, I had the unique opportunity to interview several women who were housed in various facilities. In this chapter, I have composed my interviews with these women who share their perspective about the differences in housing, programs and the structure of the Federal institutions where they were designated. From their feedback I gained quite a bit of knowledge I will share with you. It is my hope this information will be helpful in giving you an idea of what to expect from different female facilities.

Name: Patricia Morrison
Age: 44 years old
How long have you been incarcerated?
I have served 6 1/2 years on a 15 year sentence
Where have you been incarcerated?
Hazleton SFF in Hazleton, West Virginia
Alderson FPC in Alderson, West Virginia
Danbury FPC in Danbury, Connecticut

What are the differences in the programs and services that stand out to you in the Federal facilities where you have been housed?

The Education Department at Hazleton by far exceeds Danbury and Alderson's educational programs. Although Alderson has a very good education program, Hazleton stands above the others. Hazleton offered a variety of classes and did a very good job logging all the course hours into the system. I felt recognizing my efforts was very important and earning credit hours helped lower my security level so that I could eventually gain Camp status. I remember taking a really cool Science class called "Miracle Planet" where we learned about the Solar System and earned 12 course hours. I enrolled in a History class entitled "The History of Wars" and earned 10 course hours. I haven't seen classes of that variety at any other facility to date. Hazleton also offered educational programs geared toward women's issues and seminars on topics of interest to women: Breast Cancer, Diabetes, HPV, HIV/AIDS/HEPC and an especially wonderful program called 'Sistas' where a group of women get together to discuss what was important to them without judgment. The Education Department was pretty large in comparison to the other institutions I've been housed at. There were eight classrooms, many computers for inmate use and several faculty member offices. The Career Resource Center had it's own separate facility with two classrooms and two other rooms where career counseling, correspondence courses and other activities could take place.

Alderson also had a decent Education Department. The institution offers higher education classes taught by professors from local colleges and universities for which you earn college credit upon completion. On the down side, it was difficult to get into any of the classes as a new inmate because the more senior inmates received first priority. Whereas, Danbury has less original course selections and no college credit classes, enrollment is done on a lottery system so that everyone has a fair chance to take part in the classes offered.

I also rate the Recreation program at Hazleton to be second to none. They offer a modern track, a full basketball court, soccer field, softball field and an indoor gymnasium. There are available rooms where you can individually, or with a small group of ladies, pop in a work out video and exercise at your convenience. Additionally, there were separate classrooms where craft classes were held and a Recreation Room that included a pool table, televisions, foosball and ping pong tables.

Alderson also has very good vocational program offerings such as Cosmetology and Fire Fighting. The Fire Fighting program is an actual Fire Department staffed entirely of female inmates. They go out to the community to fight fires and even go to the annual Town Fair to participate in a contest against other Fire Departments. I'm not sure they ever won anything, but they got to participate and even were able to eat Fair foods while they were there.

Family Days are another reason why I think Alderson has a good Recreation program. Inmates are able to showcase their talents in a talent show held in front of inmates, their families and staff. There is a carnival atmosphere created, featuring games, cotton candy, popcorn and other activities that inmates and their families enjoy together.

The Health Services available at both Hazleton and Alderson were superior to Danbury's Health Service Department.

How would you compare housing, building, staff and overall morale within the institution?

Hazleton is overall the best compound facility. It's a new, large facility with housing separate from all other buildings and it's easy to navigate. Alderson is by far the largest compound. It's housing areas are relatively new but the other buildings were old and inundated with asbestos. There are beautiful, picturesque views of mountains on both sides with green pastures which seem to spread out for miles. It doesn't matter what time of year it is, the view is amazing! There's a log cabin that sits miles away from the Camp barely in sight in the rolling green hills. As I would see the smoke billowing out of the chimney, I would wonder who lived there and what they did. There is also a river running just behind the Camp and an Amtrak train that I looked forward to hearing as it passed through. Little things mean a lot when you're imprisoned, so taking in the view became a good way to pass the time.

Danbury also has beautiful views of Connecticut mountains, especially in the Fall season. The buildings that make up the facility are, however, the worst of the three facilities I've been housed in.

In comparing the staff and overall morale at each of the institutions, I would have to say that Danbury ranks #1. The staff is more humane and they treat inmates with some respect. In Hazleton, if you didn't cause any trouble, the staff left you alone. However, there were regular shakedowns that were annoying. In my opinion, Alderson ranks last in staff and overall morale within the institution. I always felt like I was walking on eggshells there. Shakedowns took place at least 3 times a month. I felt like my locker was this little space that was my own, holding all my belongings and it seemed like it was always being invaded. Uncomfortable is the most appropriate way to describe how I felt there.

If you were to speak with a future inmate, where would you recommend they be incarcerated? What advice would you give them?

I would recommend Danbury FPC to a future inmate, not because of the living conditions, but for peace of mind. I feel better mentally at Danbury and I've been able to grow and find myself here. I was constantly on edge at the other two institutions, but I don't feel that way at Danbury. It's likely because of the staff. Inmates come and go and I have been able to tune out those that I don't care to associate with, but you can't do that with staff.

I recommend you do what you need to do to find yourself during your incarceration. Whatever mistakes you made that brought about a Federal indictment was most likely out of character for you. Refocus on who you want to be going forward. Don't let prison get you down. There's always someone to your right or left who has it worse than you do. Yes, there will be days you're pretty sure no one has it worse, but trust me, someone always does. Reshape, remold, re-evaluate and allow your true character to prevail. You won't be disappointed. I leave you with my favorite saying - You can be anything you want to be in the BOP! Best wishes.

Name: Dorian Bess
Age: 45 years old
How long have you been incarcerated?
I've been incarcerated twice:
1997-2004 served 8 years 10 months on a 135 month sentence
2010-Present served 5 years of a 120 month sentence
Where have you been incarcerated?
First time incarcerated:
Danbury FPC in Danbury, CT
Coleman SPC in Coleman, FL
Danbury FPC in Danbury, CT
Danbury FCI in Danbury, CT
Second time incarcerated:
For 22 months I was in transit, spending time at holding centers:
MCC, New York, NY
CCA, Washington, DC
SuperMax, Baltimore, MD
Marianna SPC in Marianna, FL
Aliceville FPC in Aliceville, AL
Danbury FPC in Danbury, CT

What are the differences in the programs and services that stand out to you in the Federal facilities where you have been housed?

Truthfully, the first time I was incarcerated at Danbury FPC, and while at Marianna, there were outstanding Recreation, Education and Psychology programs in place that no longer exist at either facility. Although the Recreation Department at Danbury presently offers craft classes, there were more variety of craft classes with plenty of materials available at the time of my first incarceration. The Education Department offered college classes for credit through Marist College. This program no longer exists. Presently, there are ACE classes offered and taught by inmates, as well as RPP workshops taught by staff. But, there is not much more by way of education unless you enroll in independent study correspondence courses.

The Psychology program at Danbury previously included a team of inmates who went out to the community to speak with at-risk teens. It was a very effective program and I can't imagine why it doesn't exist any more. I think it's possible staff felt inmates were being afforded too many "luxuries" and opportunities that outside people were not being afforded; such as a college education.

Officially, we were told the reasons for losing programs such as Horticulture, Puppies in Prison and Cosmetology at Marianna were failed inspections, loss of licensing and budget shortfalls.

Aliceville claims to have a variety of programs on it's website, but in truth they don't exist. However, Aliceville does have excellent faith based programs for inmates. An inmate may earn an Associate Degree in Seminary through a local college within 2 years. Those who do not have a minimum 2-year sentence can earn a certificate in Seminary studies. As in every BOP facility, Aliceville offers the Threshold program.

I was given the opportunity to volunteer on a beautification project in the community of Aliceville. For six months, a group of inmates traveled to a local elementary school, after the 4 p.m. count each day, and worked four hour shifts to renovate the entire school. It was a wonderful opportunity to be able to travel outside of the institution and share our skills and talents to help others.

How would you compare housing, building, staff and overall morale within the institution?

The group of inmates I got off the bus with at Coleman in 1997 were given the responsibility of opening this brand new facility. We put beds together, laid concrete for the basketball court, set up Commissary, Food Service and Laundry. We were paid $120 for our services, which is considered very good for prison wages. In comparison, for the same work we performed at Aliceville, we were paid only $5.25.

Aliceville, was also a brand new facility when I arrived there. I always felt the newly hired staff was using the inmates for their training. Consequently, they constantly patted us down and performed shakedowns regularly. The Warden was "standoffish" as well.

The dorms have an 'open bay' set up where approximately 250 woman are housed. There are no cubicles or partitions, therefore, there is no privacy. It is structured much like a holding or state facility where I've been housed before. To new inmates, this setting is difficult to deal with due to the lack of privacy.

At Coleman, the facility was brand new, but the staff was seasoned. Coleman is housed on a compound with 5 other facilities, so the staff was rotated among the facilities. The Warden at Coleman was the BEST! He regularly allowed the Choir and Praise Team to go out on furloughs to visit nursing homes and schools to perform. He also allowed inmate visits between institutions with immediate family members and spouses, as long as both inmates were in good standing. He allowed furloughs so that inmates could attend their children's high school and college graduation ceremonies. Additionally, he compassionately allowed bedside and funeral visits to immediate family who were terminally ill. The Camp Administrator and Counselor, along with the rest of the staff, were caring, nurturing people as well. It was a laid back, relaxed atmosphere where you never saw inmates in conflict with each other.

Both Aliceville and Coleman have equal Recreation facilities. Everything was state of the art and brand new.

Marianna holds approximately 400 women and also has a laid back, relaxed atmosphere. There were two UNICOR facilities there, however, one has recently closed. UNICOR, at that time, employed nearly half of the inmate population. I can't tell you a lot about Marianna's facilities because I worked all the time while there. I was one of the Head Clerks at UNICOR, a very responsible and time consuming position, so I didn't get much of a chance to take advantage of the facilities.

If you were to speak with a future inmate, where would you recommend they be incarcerated? What advice would you give them?

I would tell them "Don't commit a crime. Stay out of prison." But, seriously, I like structure and a place that enforces rules, makes offenders aware of the mistakes they've made and provides services to allow inmates to better themselves. I like a comfortable, harassment free environment. In Marianna, rules weren't enforced as they should have been. There are also a lot of inconsistencies in rule enforcement in Aliceville and Danbury, so Coleman would be my recommendation.

If you are given the opportunity to be designated to a facility, stay at the facility. Transit to another BOP facility can take weeks or months and is difficult. I was in transit for almost two years, housed temporarily in holding centers in New York, DC and Maryland before I was finally sent to Florida.

My advice would be to look to your faith while incarcerated. Get your education, your GED or a college education, and do whatever it takes. Get involved in self-help programs and advocate for programs you're interested in that don't exist. Get involved! Keep your mind occupied and forget about what's going on in the outside world because you can't do anything about it!

Name: Barbara Davis
Age: 55 years old
How long have you been incarcerated?

I've been incarcerated since 1997 and have served 17 years of a 30 year sentence.

Where have you been incarcerated?

Geiger FPC in Geiger, WA for 2 1/2 months until they shut it down and converted it to a state facility in 1998.

Phoenix FPC in Phoenix, AZ for two years.

Dublin FPC in Dublin, CA for three years. (I transferred for RDAP. This facility was shut down in July, 2014 for failure to pass an ACA accreditation.)

Dublin FCI in Dublin, CA for 10 years. The BOP, in it's infinite wisdom, decided that I wasn't eligible for Camp status. I must point out to you here the lack of communication and attention given to individual cases in the Federal system. I was incarcerated for 4 years before it was discovered that I was not eligible to serve my time in an FPC.

Danbury FPC in Danbury, CT is where I am currently housed.

CHAPTER 12: FEMALE OFFENDERS QUESTIONS & ANSWERS (Q&A)

What are the differences in the programs and services that stand out to you in the Federal facilities where you have been housed?

In Dublin FCI I was one of the founders of Getting Out by Going In (GOGI). The program had been offered at Terminal Island, a men's Federal facility, but had never been offered in any female Federal facility. I was proud to be a pioneer of this program. this program, founded by Maria Taylor as a non-profit organization and completely funded by donations. In the GOGI program, inmates are taught the 12 tools to make positive changes in their lives. I've completed LifeSkills, RDAP and several other programs, but this was the most life changing program I've been a part of thus far. I plan to advocate for this program to be offered at Danbury FPC, where I am currently housed. I earned a level 6 coach certification in GOGI, making me eligible to teach inside and outside of an institutional setting.

At Dublin, Phoenix and Danbury, I taught many craft programs. Dublin and Phoenix were very organized programs that revolved around the choices of the inmates. I was given more than ample resources needed to teach entertaining and productive craft classes. At Danbury, the crafts program seems to revolve around what resources are available after the larger male facility on the same property is served. Generally, in the BOP, men have more access to a variety of resources and craft classes such as leather making, bead work and welding. I know this because I communicate with my husband regularly who is serving a life sentence at Florence, Colorado Penitentiary.

Phoenix offered an employment program for inmates outside of the BOP. There were jobs in the community as landscape technicians for a local trailer park and museum. There was also a UNICOR facility on site that produced electronic parts. I took advantage of the higher wages offered because I didn't have any outside financial support.

How would you compare housing, building, staff and overall morale within the institution?

I can't say much about Geiger because I was only there 2 1/2 months. It's now a state facility.

At Phoenix FPC I felt most inmates were content and happy. There were very few fights and mostly everyone got along with each other. Staff were respectful, but we only saw them every 3-4 hours because they were responsible for four units that housed 350 inmates, and the units were not in close proximity.

The facility was well cared for from the landscaping to the interiors of the buildings. Inmates shared two person cubicles separated by cement half walls. There were bunk beds, a desk, two tall lockers for clothing and items, and two small food lockers.

Because of the location of this facility, there were many Spanish-Americans incarcerated at Phoenix FPC. Since there was no national BOP menu at the time, food service catered to the largest group and served mostly Southwestern and Mexican entrees.

Dublin FPC was condemned and closed in July, 2014 at the recommendation of the American Correctional Accreditation Committee. Truthfully, I thought the living conditions were better at Dublin then at Danbury. There were two floors of three units on a former military base. The building we were housed in was a former POW holding area made completely of wood. We always worried about a fire and how we would escape from that old building with it's narrow steps. In hindsight, I imagine the potential fire and safety hazard is one of the reasons why the Camp was condemned. We shared four person cubicles containing bunk beds, lockers, one very large desk and individual wall mounted bulletin boards.

The staff at Dublin FPC were approachable and decent people. There was an unwritten policy to "Police your own." If an inmate went to a staff member with a minor problem, they would say "Police yourselves." They were mostly concerned about major violations.

In my opinion, Dublin FCI had the best inmate living conditions. Housing is separate from the other buildings, but you could walk to where you needed to go within the 10 minute move period. The building used for housing is a glass, symmetrically sloped, 2-story structure. It contains six housing units with giant TV rooms in each lobby, as well as TV rooms in the units. Everything seemed to be GIANT there - giant building, giant TV rooms, giant microwaves, giant ice machine, giant washing machines and dryers. Inmates were responsible for their own laundry at Dublin and at every facility I've been housed in with the exception of Danbury.

The dorm-like rooms were shared by three inmates. There was an entrance door, toilet and sink within each room. If you asked for privacy from your bunkies, it was always granted. Unlike Danbury, where it's difficult to find a quiet work area, there are two reading/study rooms that were always quiet at Dublin.

The staff at Dublin also adhered to the "Police your own" unofficial policy. If you didn't bother them, they didn't bother you. There was peace among the inmates with very little disturbances.

For recreation, there was a roller skating rink (which has since been removed), tennis courts, handball, basketball, indoor and outdoor volleyball courts, outside weight pavilion, one 1/4 mile track and one 1/3 mile track.

Dublin supports two UNICOR facilities at both the Camp and FCI. Camp UNICOR assembles office furniture and the FCI UNICOR previously employed inmates to be 411 telephone operators. However, when that contract was terminated, inmates performed telemarketing work.

If you were to speak with a future inmate, where would you recommend they be incarcerated? What advice would you give them?

I would recommend Dublin FCI because of the educational and vocational opportunities. I kept busy there and the time went by quickly. There wasn't any nonsense and I was never bored. If you wanted to keep busy at Dublin FCI, you could. At Danbury, there is turmoil, possibly from the lack of things to do. The programs and services are unimaginative and there are little resources available as compared to other institutions. All these factors combined fuels inmate apathy.

My advice to a future inmate is to keep your head down, mouth shut and hands in you pockets. This too shall pass. Keep yourself busy. There's no reason to be bitter, depressed or angry. Do your time with dignity and move forward when you're done. You can learn from doing time inside and use it to your benefit on the outside.

Name: Carrie Denniston
Age: 41 years old
How long have you been incarcerated?
From 2009 - Present
I have served nearly 6 years on a 13 1/2 year sentence.
Where have you been incarcerated?
Waseca FCI in Waseca, MN
Lexington FPC in Lexington, KY
Danbury FPC in Danbury, CT

What are the differences in the programs and services that stand out to you in the Federal facilities where you have been housed?

Overall, the programs and services offered at Waseca FCI stand out above the two Camp facilities to me. Education is very important at Waseca. The staff make it a high priority and they devote time to ensuring inmates have access to desirable educational programs, because they believe education contributes to positive rehabilitation. I completed many ACE classes in a short period of time mostly because they were offered as video courses. The subjects ranged from Jazz to National Geographic topics. At the conclusion of an ACE class and after successful completion of a Post test, Sentry credit was awarded. Accumulating Sentry credit contributes to eventually earning Camp status. Also at Waseca FCI, there are many Wellness Education programs taught by both inmates and staff. I participated in classes such as Heart & Healthy and Zumba Fitness. Not only did I enjoy the fitness and learning aspects of each program, I also had fun! I was fortunate to participate in the Horticulture Program where we planted flowers in rows on an unused soccer field. I was in charge of the Sunflower Row. Due to this experience, I am now under the belief that the smell of flowers can cure what ails you. I enjoyed the time outdoors, the learning experience and the camaraderie.

The outdoor Recreation area at Waseca FCI reminded me of a rest stop for travelers that you find alongside major highways. The fitness center, benches, paved track, softball field, volleyball courts and badminton area were perfectly placed in a beautifully landscaped area dotted with benches and picnic tables. In the Recreation area, there is even a Native American sweat lodge. Cameras line the landscape, but don't take away from the aesthetics.

Although I am not eligible for the RDAP program for a few years, it is available at Waseca FCI. I have already been accepted to RDAP at Greenville FPC in Illinois which places me closer to home.

I would be remiss if I didn't mention the PAWS program available to inmates as a job assignment at Waseca. I can't quite remember what PAWS is an acronym for, but I do know that inmates in this program train service dogs to assist disabled people. If you're like me, this is a great opportunity to earn money and enjoy the animals.

At Lexington FPC, there's not much that stands out to me in programs and services available except for the Second Chance Dog program. Dogs are chosen from animal shelters and inmates train them in manners so that their chances of adoption are greatly increased.

I worked a lot during my time at Lexington FPC because there wasn't much to be involved in. I don't believe I took any classes while there or got involved in any programs like I did at Waseca FCI.

I transferred on a furlough to Danbury FPC this year to take part in the Puppies Behind Bars program. A furlough to travel to another institution independently rather than utilizing "Con Air," is a reward I was granted because I had no shots and no incident reports during the whole time I've been incarcerated. Therefore, I was trusted enough to travel on my own. I previously transferred from Waseca to Kentucky on a furlough and was given $40 and a bus ticket. However, the bus schedule didn't quite work out for me. It ended up taking two days to get there when it should have only taken one. I promptly called the Camp where I was heading and ended up spending many hours hanging out at a Wal-Mart nearby. I wasn't complaining because it felt like freedom. My second furlough to get to Danbury worked out well. I was given $20 this time and a bus ticket to get myself there. In the Puppies Behind Bars program, I am being taught to train dogs to be Explosive Detection Canines (EDC). Although the program is all consuming, it's not a paying job, so I work in the Electrical Shop to earn my much needed spending money for Commissary, telephone and computer use. However, I will earn an Apprenticeship certificate from the Department of Labor after approximately two years or 4,000 hours of training and instruction. After two years, I may choose to remain in the program.

Other than the beautiful views, Danbury has nothing more to offer me by way of Education or Recreation programs. In my opinion, there are not a lot of resources available to run any of the programs effectively. However, they do have the Puppies in Prison program, so I know where I will want to be for at least the next two years.

How would you compare housing, building, staff and overall morale within the institution?

Waseca FCI is situated on a former college Campus. There are 2500 women housed in five units. RDAP and PAWS program account for two housing units. The housing areas are in 'Open Bus Stop' style separated by lockers. There are up to 16 and as little as two inmates per bus stop. Although the housing units are separated from all the other buildings, you can get to everything in the allotted 10 minute moves, which occur each hour on the hour. During 10 minute moves, inmates have ten minutes to get where they need to go before all the doors in each area are locked. Center Hall housed the Chow Hall, Commissary, Medical, Psychology and Laundry in the middle of the Campus. There is a pathway from there that leads to CMS, Education and UNICOR, where workers make military clothing and perform sewing services. The Recreation building is the furthest building away from the housing units, but can still be reached within the 10 minute move periods.

The staff is very professional, more professional than any other facility I've been housed in. They treated inmates with respect and they were always given respect in return. Overall morale was high when I was there.

Lexington FPC houses approximately 250 female inmates in an old 3-story brick building with an elevator. The Garage, Warehouse and UNICOR, where inmates manufacture electrical cords, are separate from the housing.

The FPC was once a Narcotic Farm where celebrities like Elvis Presley and Johnny Cash came for drug addiction rehabilitation. There are ghosts that live in the housing area; the most popular one is named Henry. It's a historical place that you can read about in a book titled "Narcotic Farm" by Nancy D. Campbell. I can describe to you all day my experiences with Henry and the other ghosts, but read the book; I'm sure you'll enjoy it.

The rest of the compound in Lexington includes an FMC for men that formerly housed women. It's like a city within a city. The female housing is also set up as 'bus stops,' housing 2 - 4 inmates per stop with shared bathrooms. There was one room that had it's own bathroom with shower. It was a real treat to be assigned to that room.

The first floor of the 3-story building was referred to by inmates as "Medical Alley." It's where the Medical Department and Church are located, but also the elderly and physically handicapped inmates are housed there. If inmates need medical attention that can not be provided on Campus, they are taken to Kentucky University Hospital for treatment, escorted by a CO. This differs from Danbury FPC where a inmate employed as the Town Driver may escort you to medical appointments off Campus.

Lexington has a mansion on Campus where the Warden resides, and like Danbury FPC, staff housing available for government employees who choose to live on Campus. There is also a Recreation area and a Pavilion where 'Town Hall' meetings take place. To me, Lexington was not as nice as Waseca.

From my experience at Camps, the staff are generally inconsistent in enforcing rules. I feel that FCIs are the only place where rules are strictly adhered to. Camps tend to provide a more laid back atmosphere; some more than others. The overall morale at Lexington FPC was low and I would not recommend you do your time there.

Danbury FPC, where I am presently housed is overall a decent place to be, but not as good as Waseca. There is a very nice, scenic outdoor area with a track and fitness center, but the fitness equipment and the track are in disrepair. The staff is not professional and are very inconsistent, worse than Lexington FPC, with enforcing the rules. I find that some staff are too militant, like they are at an FCI, not a Camp, and others are very laid back. I think that some may be confusing their position with an FCI staff position since the staff interchanges duties at the adjacent men's FCI facility.

If you were to speak with a future inmate, where would you recommend they be incarcerated? What advice would you give them?

If you must be incarcerated, I would recommend Waseca as the place to be housed because of the consistency of rules and good programs, especially the PAWS program. Days go by quickly there because there are a lot of activities to participate in. It's also the cleanest and best kept facility I've been housed at.

My advice is to do your time, don't let the time do you. Stay active, get outside and don't worry about what anyone else is doing. Take advantage of any program and information you can utilize on the outside. Good Luck :)

Name: Janel Doyle
Age: 36 years old
How long have you been incarcerated?
I have served 30 months on a 4 year sentence
Where have you been incarcerated?
Tallahassee FCI in Tallahassee, Florida
Danbury FPC in Danbury, Connecticut

What are the differences in the programs and services that stand out to you in the Federal facilities where you have been housed?

Danbury FPC does not compare to the Education Department and Career Resource Center at Tallahassee; Tallahassee is second to none. There are Vocational Training (VT) courses offered in fields such as Business, Cosmetology, Horticulture and Building Trades. These vocational courses are accredited by the Council on Occupational Education. A certificate is issued by the Commission on Occupational Education Institutions upon completion of all competencies in each course of study. In Business, I completed 12 courses including Business Math, Business English, Words @ Work, Office Procedures & Technology, Mavis Beacon Typing, Introduction to Business, Practical Internet, Business Law and Video Professor courses on Word, Excel and PowerPoint to earn my certificate. ACE courses are also offered in such areas as Foreign Languages - French, Italian and Spanish, Business - Budgeting and Money Management as well as Basic Law and Electronic Law Library. Courses are taught by inmates as well as outside instructors and can be taken concurrent with VT courses. Unlike Danbury FPC where an inmate may only be enrolled in one class per cycle.

The Recreation Department at Tallahassee provides a variety of activities to the 1200 inmates housed there. There is a softball field, volleyball and outdoor racquetball, which can be utilized all year because of the Florida climate. From April through June, inmates participate in the "Battle of the Units" and compete against each other in activities like football, fitness, volleyball, chess, pool, ping pong and Biggest Loser. The winners were treated to a movie, cake and ice cream.

With approximately 200 inmates housed at Danbury FPC, little resources, creativity and thought are put into the Recreation programs.

How would you compare housing, building, staff and overall morale within the institution?

The housing units at Tallahassee are 'open bay' cubicles separated by very short walls giving the bottom bunk privacy but affording the top bunk none. There are four inmates per bay with four lockers double stacked in the middle of the cubicle. With the exception of one or two hooks on the wall, there is no other storage space. Danbury offers under-bed totes and unlimited wall hooks to store items, which allows for a neater living space.

The compound at Tallahassee is triangle shaped with five buildings on the same level as the housing units - Food Service, Medical, Commissary, Chapel, Lieutenant Office and Upper Recreation. Slightly down hill are the Safety, Psychology, Education, Laundry, Food Service Warehouse, Facilities, Rec Yard and UNICOR buildings. The UNICOR at Tallahassee employs inmates in the telemarketing field. Prior to March, 2014, inmates performed the function of 411 operators.

Danbury FPC is one long hallway with new arrival rooms, offices, classrooms, tv/visiting room, recreation room, and Career Resource Center on one floor and three dorms on the lower floor. With the exception of the Commissary, Warehouse, Fitness Center, UNICOR and CMS, everything is in one building.

The staff at Tallahassee treated the inmates the same as at Danbury, which is unorganized and inconsistent. I thought the COs at Tallahassee were rookies who were learning their job as they went along and that's what caused the inconsistency. I was as comfortable at that facility as I am at Danbury. There aren't a lot of shakedowns at either facility, however,

Tallahassee staff were concerned with inmates taking food out of the kitchen, so we were often patted down.

It is difficult for me to assess the morale at a facility as large as Tallahassee. With 1200 inmates, there's going to be good and bad days. Overall, the morale is good at Danbury, but I haven't spent the winter season here yet.

If you were to talk to a future inmate, where would you recommend they be incarcerated and what advice would you give them?

I would recommend Danbury FPC because it's a Camp with more freedom. At Tallahassee, when inmates were Camp status they could obtain Gate Passes to work outside the gate in the Landscaping, Garage and Out Maintenance Departments, but that's all the freedom we were afforded.

My advice to a future inmate would be to stay positive, stay busy, stay focused and start your plan for post release from your first day of incarceration. I wish you well.

KEY TERMS AND DEFINITIONS

EXPLOSIVE DETECTION CANINES (EDC) - Also known as the 'Puppies Behind Bars' program where dogs are trained to detect explosives for the the U.S. Government.

FURLOUGH - An authorized absence from an institution by an inmate who is not under escort of a BOP staff member, U.S. Marshall, State or Federal Agent.

RELEASE PREPARATION PROGRAM (RPP) - A series of workshops offered in all BOP institutions and required for inmates to be considered for RRC placement or home confinement.

THRESHOLD PROGRAM - A 6-month spirituality based program offered in the BOP through Chaplaincy Services.

TOWN DRIVER - An inmate driver position with the responsibility of running errands for prison officials and transporting low security inmates outside of the facility.

Chapter 13

Transfers, Furloughs and Methods to Gain A Speedy Release

The Beginning of the End!

By: Jamila T. Davis

It is common for inmates within the BOP to be designated far away from their homes. This makes visiting and maintaining family ties extremely difficult. In this chapter, we will explore ways to obtain a transfer closer to home and the requirements to be granted a furlough.

If you are anything like me, the main questions you want to know as a new inmate is how much time you will have to serve and, how you can get out sooner? Because of our desperation to escape the gruesome wrath of incarceration, many inmates become easy targets of legal scams. It is likely you will receive mail from numerous legal service companies that will claim they can help get you out of prison early, but beware! Many of these companies use deceptive marketing tactics to entice those of us behind bars, often after receiving hefty retainers, little to no legal work is performed on the inmates' behalf.

In this chapter, I will also share with you information on BOP procedures for release and inform you about available options that can reduce the time you serve in prison. Utilizing this information, you will be equipped to navigate through federal prison and gain an early release!

TRANSFER REQUEST

You can go to your Case Manager at any time to request a transfer to another institution. Some institutions require you maintain clean conduct for at least 18 months prior to requesting a transfer. If you are more than 500 miles away from your home, you may have a good chance of receiving a transfer. You may also request a transfer to attend any national program such as RDAP, the Faith Program or the Puppies Behind Bars Program. At times certain institutions will offer inmates a transfer to attend a specific program they are offering. You can ask your Case Manager about these available programs. If you consent, your paperwork will be reviewed and if you qualify for the program, your transfer will be processed.

If you are a high security inmate, you can attend programs and classes that will reduce your security level. In that case, when your security level is reduced, you can request a transfer to another facility.

FURLOUGH REQUEST

A furlough is an authorized absence from an institution by an inmate who is not under escort of a BOP staff member, U.S. Marshal, State or Federal Agent.

According to the BOP Program Statement, Statue 570.33, "the Warden or designee may authorize a furlough, for 30 calendar days or less, for an inmate to:

1. Transfer directly to another Bureau institution, a non-federal facility, or community confinement;
2. Be present during a crisis in the immediate family, or in other urgent situations;
3. Participate in the development of release plans;
4. Establish or re-establish family and community ties;
5. Participate in selected educational, social, civic, and religious activities, which will facilitate release transition;
6. Appear in Court in connection with a civil action;
7. Comply with an official request to appear before a grand jury, or to comply with a request from a legislative body, or regulatory or licensing agency.
8. Appear in or prepare for a criminal court proceeding, but only when the use of a furlough is requested or recommended by the applicable court or prosecuting attorney;

9. Participate in special training courses or in institution work assignments including Federal Prison Industries (FPI) work assignments, when daily commuting from the institution is not feasible; or
10. Receive necessary medical, surgical, psychiatric or dental treatment not otherwise available at the facility where housed.

If an inmate has been confined for less than 90 days or has more than two years remaining until the projected release date, he or she is only eligible for an emergency furlough. If an inmate has two years or less remaining until the projected release date, he or she is eligible for an emergency furlough or routine day furlough. If an inmate has 18 months or less remaining until the projected release date, he or she is generally eligible for an emergency furlough, a routine day furlough, or a routine overnight furlough within the institution's community area. If an inmate has less than a year until the projected release date, he or she may take advantage of all furlough options, including a routine overnight furlough either within or outside the institution's community area.

All expenses of a furlough, including transportation, food, lodging and incidentals are the responsibility of the inmate, the inmate's family, or other appropriate source approved by the Warden. The only exception is if the furlough is for the government's primary benefit, then the government will cover the expense. Inmates will be thoroughly searched and given a urinalysis, breathalyzer, and other comparable test upon their return, for which the inmate is required to pay, unless the furlough is for the primary benefit of the government.

If you are a low level inmate and you meet the above requirements, you can fill out a furlough application and submit it to your Counselor for review. Please note, each institution may vary on it's furlough approval process. You can inquire with staff, and other inmates who may have been granted furloughs, about your institution's eligibility process.

GOOD TIME CALCULATION

As previously discussed, there is no such thing as Federal parole for inmates sentenced after November 1, 1987, in accordance with the Sentencing Reform Act of 1984 (SRA). Under the SRA, the only good time available for all federal inmates is 54 days of Good Conduct Time (GCT) for each year served on a sentence. There is no good time allotted for prisoners who are serving life terms, or to those serving a year or less. Additionally, GCT is not awarded under the SRA until the end of each year served on the sentence, and may be awarded in a part or whole as GCT is dependent upon the behavior of the individual. If you do not receive any incident reports and remain in compliance with BOP Education requirements, your GCT is secure. Once awarded, GCT time can not be later taken away.

RELEASE DATES

When you arrive to prison and attend your first Unit Team meeting, you will be given two dates. The furthest date is your projected release date. That is the estimated date you will be released from prison with your GCT. You will also be given a Home Confinement/Home Detention date. That is the estimated date that you will be eligible to serve the remainder of your sentence on home confinement.

HOME CONFINEMENT/DETENTION

Home confinement or home detention gives federal prisoners the ability to serve the last 10% of their sentence, up to six months, in their own home. During this period, the prisoner is still under the authority of the BOP. He or she is required to keep a curfew and demonstrate the ability to pay for food and medical expenses.

While serving time on home confinement, an inmate who is under the supervision of a halfway house is required to pay 25% of their gross income to the residence where they were housed. If the inmate goes directly to home confinement, and if under the direct supervision of the U.S. Probation, he or she may only have to pay the monthly monitoring system fee, which is approximately $100/per month.

While on home confinement, a prisoner may be required to work and must meet drug treatment programming requirements. Those serving a home confinement term may also be required to wear an electronic device that allows the BOP to track their movements. If the inmate goes outside of his or her restricted area, the person could be subject to an escape charge.

It is important to note the BOP does not always allow a person the privilege of being released to home confinement for the remaining 10% of their sentence. Inmates who are deemed by the BOP to be a higher risk for failure may require more re-entry services and may be denied home confinement.

RESIDENTIAL RE-ENTRY CENTER PLACEMENT

Inmates who are nearing release and who need assistance in obtaining a job, residence or other community resources, may be referred for placement at a Residential Re-Entry Center (RRC). An RRC, also known as a "Halfway House," is a community transitional home. The RRC has structured programs, job placement services and counseling for residents. They also provide drug testing, counseling and alcohol monitoring or treatment.

RRCs are called "Halfway Houses" because you are considered halfway free, being granted the ability to work in the community and obtain passes to go home! Many former inmates complain about the strict rules of RRCs, because it is a smaller environment and residents are constantly monitored even when they go out into the community. It is typical for the RRC to call the work place or residence of inmates several times daily to ensure they are actually in their authorized designation.

While housed in an RRC, all residents are required to pay 25% of their gross income to the RRC for housing. If the inmate has remained free of incident reports and has successfully gained employment, he or she may be released early into home confinement at the discretion of the manager of the RRC. During this period, the inmate is still required to pay 25% of his or her gross income and may be required to check into the RRC several times a week.

The advantage of being at an RRC is the ability to be close to home and interact in the free world, yet inmates must adhere to the rules. If not, they risk violating and being sent back to prison.

WAYS TO GAIN AN EARLY RELEASE

As previously discussed, there are only a few ways to gain relief from the Courts and your sentence overturned or reduced. In this chapter segment, we will discuss the ways in which you may be released early without going through the U.S. Courts.

EXTENDED RRC PLACEMENT - According to the Second Chance Act, inmates in need can apply to receive up to 12 months in an RRC. Typically, inmates receive up to six months of RRC time, but you can request additional time. The key to receiving additional time is you MUST be in real need of assistance in getting re-established.

The RRC provides assistance to those who need help finding a job, locating a residence and re-establishing family ties. Therefore, you will need to show you require additional help in at least one of these areas to be considered for extra halfway house time.

If you would like additional information about RRC Placement policy see Memorandum For Chief Executive Officers, Revised Guidance For Residential Re-entry Center, 6/24/2010, located at the end of this chapter.

RDAP PROGRAM - RDAP is an intensive drug abuse treatment program offered to inmates who have been diagnosed with a drug use disorder. For nine months, participants are housed together in a segregated area where they participate in a 500-hour residential program. Qualifying inmates who successfully complete the 500-hour course are granted up to 12 months off their sentence.

To qualify for RDAP, you must have at least 24 months left to serve on your sentence, have a verifiable substance-use disorder, be willing to participate in the program and sign a statement accepting responsibility for the obligations of the program and be able to complete all phases of the RDAP program including the community-based component.

Before you can be considered for the RDAP program, the Drug Abuse Program Coordinator must be able to verify that you had a substance-use disorder twelve months prior to your arrest for the instant offense. This information can be verified through your PSR. If it is not in your PSR, you can seek documentation from a substance abuse treatment provider where you previously received treatment. This document must have been written at the time services were provided and must demonstrate that a substance use diagnosis was completed at the time you were seen. Additionally, this document must show that treatment was provided for that documented substance abuse diagnosis.

Documentation to verify a substance use disorder can also be provided from a probation officer, a parole officer, a social services professional, etc., who has information that verifies your problem with illegal or illicit substances.

If you can not produce this documentation, you may show physical proof of your substance use by consenting to be examined by medical staff. Physical proof would include track marks, abscesses, etc. Or, if you received substance detoxification as you entered prison, you may sign a consent form for the drug treatment staff to verify your detoxification with Health Services.

After your substance use is verified, you will be referred to the Drug Abuse Program Coordinator for a diagnostic interview.

Participating in RDAP will get you an early release as long as you do not have any prior felony or misdemeanor convictions for homicide, forcible rape, robbery, arson, kidnapping, aggravated assault, or child sexual abuse offenses. In addition, your current conviction can not: (1) have an element of actual, attempted, or threatened use of physical force against the person or property of another (2) involve the carrying, possession, or use of a firearm or other dangerous weapon or explosives (3) present a serious potential risk of physical force against the person or property of another (4) involve sexual abuse offenses committed upon minors.

EXECUTIVE CLEMENCY - The President of the United States is authorized under the Constitution to grant executive clemency by pardon, commutation of sentence, or reprieve.

A pardon is an executive act of grace that is a symbol of forgiveness. It does not connote innocence nor does it expunge the record of conviction. However, a pardon restores civil rights and facilitates the restoration of professional and other licenses that may have been lost by reason of the conviction. You can not apply for a pardon until at least five years from the date of your release from confinement.

A commutation of sentence is usually the last chance an inmate has to correct injustice, which has occurred in the criminal justice process. Based on your case and your circumstances, the President may commute your sentence. Your Unit Team has the necessary forms to apply for commutation. Please note, a commutation of sentence is very rare, yet that should not stop you from seeking relief.

A reprieve is the suspension of execution of a sentence for a period of time. The President has the power to stay a sentence if he sees fit. Seek the assistance of your attorney to make application for this relief.

COMPASSIONATE RELEASE/REDUCTION IN SENTENCE - The Director of the BOP may make a motion to an inmate's sentencing Court for a reduction in sentence under extraordinary and compelling circumstances, in accordance with 18 U.S.C.S. 3582 and Program Statement on Compassionate Release/Reduction in Sentence.

According to the BOP Statement, request for Compassionate Release may be granted for both medical and non-medical circumstances.

Medical circumstances for compassionate release may be considered for:
1. inmates who have been diagnosed with a terminal, incurable disease and whose life expectancy is eighteen months or less, or
2. inmates who have an incurable, progressive illness or who have suffered a debilitating injury from which they will not recover.

Non-medical circumstances for Compassionate Release may be considered for:
1. elderly inmates who are 70 years or older, sentenced under the new law (imposed November 1, 1987) and have served 30 years or more on their term of imprisonment.
2. elderly inmates who are 65 years or older, suffer from chronic or serious medical conditions related to the aging process, experience deteriorating mental or physical health that substantially diminishes their ability to function in a correctional facility and have served at least 50% of their sentence.

3. elderly inmates age 65 or older who have served the greater of 10 years or 75% of the term of imprisonment to when the inmate was sentenced.
4. inmates who have experienced the death or incapacitation of a family member, during incarceration, who was the sole caregiver for the inmate's child.

If you meet the qualifications above you may fill out a request for Compassionate Release through your Unit Team. Please note, Compassionate Releases are rarely given. Therefore, make sure you have all of the documentation you need to present a compelling case.

RELEASE PREPARATION PROGRAM (RPP)

All inmates within 24 months of their release are required to participate in the Release Preparation Program (RPP). To be considered for RRC placement or home confinement you need to be in compliance with RPP requirements. The RPP program consists of attending six mandatory workshops that last about an hour each. These workshops include:

RE1 - Health & Nutrition
RN2 - Employment - Interview Techniques
RN3 - Personal Finance - Balancing a Checkbook
RN4 - Community Resources - Community Corrections Visit
RN5 - Release Requirements - Methods of Release
RN6 - Personal Growth - Personal Growth & Development

It is my suggestion you inquire about the schedules when these workshops will take place in your institution and request to be placed on the Call Out to attend by submitting a Cop Out to your Case Manager. Participation looks good on your Team papers and will keep you in compliance to receive RRC and home confinement consideration.

CHAPTER 13: THE BEGINNING OF THE END!

RRC REQUEST

Approximately 18 months from your projected release date, your Case Manager will begin to prepare your RRC request, also called "Halfway House Package." Your personal information is gathered to be assessed by the Residential Re-entry Manager (RRM) for determination of how much halfway house or home confinement time you will receive. Based on your re-entry needs and your Unit Team's recommendation, the RRM determines a home confinement or halfway house release date.

As a part of this process, your file is sent to the U.S. Probation Department that presides over the area in which you reside. The probation officer will generally perform a home visit during this process to determine if your residence is suitable. This process can be delayed if you have changed your address to a location outside of your former district. In this instance a relocation request has to go out to the U.S. Probation office over the area you will now reside, and the Probation Department in the new District has to accept you. Please note, the relocation process can take several months. Therefore, if you decide to move, you should notify your Case Manager immediately, and request a relocation. Make sure you follow up to ensure that is was done and you were accepted. If not, it can delay your release!

Additionally, make sure your home has suitable living space and is in a presentable condition. If there are other felons living in the home, other than your spouse, who are also on supervised release or probation, your residence may be denied. Once Probation approves your residence, the approval is forwarded to the RRM. If all your documents are in order, shortly after, you will receive a date.

I have been housed with many inmates who have had problems obtaining a date. In many instances, their halfway house packages did not go out in time or they waited too late to do a relocation. It is my advice, within 18 months of your release date you make sure your halfway house package is submitted. You will know when it's been processed because you will be called in to sign your papers. If you are not called in within 18 months of your release, inquire about the process with your Case Manager. Always be courteous and respectful. I've witnessed a Case Manager purposely hold up the release of inmates who she felt were bothersome. Additionally, it is the

Case Manager who recommends the length of your halfway house or home confinement time. Therefore, be cautious and pleasant, yet remain proactive.

PREPARING FOR RELEASE

Once you are called in by your Case Manager and given a date, you are nearing your release and you must prepare! Start getting rid of excess belongings and ship your important papers home.

Expect to be called by medical to give your DNA, which is required by law to be on file. Your fingerprints will once again be taken and you will be required to verify travel arrangements. If someone is coming to pick you up, the person will need to be an approved visitor on your visiting list. In addition, you will need to provide the license plate number, the year, the make and the model of the car you will drive out in.

A month prior to your departure, you can request to fill out a clothing form. This form will allow your family to send your clothes for your release. Be sure to inquire about the exact items that can be sent in. If anything is extra in the package that is not authorized, the entire package will be sent back!

The day before you are released, you will do what is called a "Merry-Go-Round." You take a sheet obtained from your Unit Team around to specific departments to gain a signature that shows you are in compliance with the department for release. This process verifies you have returned all items from the department before your departure.

The morning of your release, you will be required to report to R&D. The R&D staff member will process you out, verify your identity and give you a debit card that holds the remainder of the balance in your Commissary account. Additionally, indigent inmates will be provided travel tickets and up to $500.00 for expenses.

Generally, if you are going home on home confinement or to a halfway house, you will be given a specific amount of hours to get to your location. Be sure you get to your destination on time or risk violation. Additionally, make sure you travel to your destination in the approved vehicle. Traveling a different way can also get you violated!

If you are going to a halfway house, it is my advice you request the handbook for that particular halfway house prior to your arrival. Some halfway house handbooks are available on the TRULINCS system for download or you may submit a Cop Out to the Re-entry Director at the institution where you are housed to obtain a copy. Familiarize yourself with the rules and regulations and be sure to follow them.

If you are going home on home detention, be sure to know your Probation Officer's information and give him or her a call immediately upon your release so you will remain in compliance.

Those exiting prison on their actual release date and serving time on supervised release have 48 hours from the time of release to check in with U.S. Probation. Be sure to check in on time so you will be in compliance!

SUPERVISED RELEASE

Once you are out of BOP custody, the worst is over! Supervised release isn't that bad for people who follow the rules. In the beginning you may be required to report once a week until your Probation Officer (PO) gets to know you and you have secured employment. Once you have a job or enroll in school full time, you will be called in less often. As long as you pay your fines and restitution, you will eventually only have to report once a month or every other month. The key to doing time on probation is to remain low key and stay out of trouble!

HOW TO GET OFF SUPERVISED RELEASE EARLY

After serving a year on supervised release either you or your attorney can submit a motion for Termination of Supervised Release in accordance with 18. U.S.C.S. 3583 (e) (1). This statute states: The Court may "terminate a term of supervised release and discharge the defendant released at any time after the expiration of one year of supervised release to the provisions of the Federal Rules of Common Procedure relating to the modification of probation if it is satisfied that such action is warranted by the conduct of the defendant released and the interest of justice."

It is my recommendation that you develop a good rapport with your PO. Just before you submit a motion for Termination of Supervised Release, let your PO know of your intent. If he or she supports you getting off early, it will bolster your chances of the motion being granted. Additionally, it would be good to show that you are working and involved in community outreach programs. It is your goal to show the Judge you are now a law abiding citizen who no longer requires supervision and will stay out of trouble.

CONCLUSION

You worked hard to get to this point. Don't mess it up! Utilize the lessons you've learned to help you succeed in life. Successfully completing your prison term will make you realize the power of your inner strength. If you can overcome the obstacle of imprisonment, chances are you can overcome anything! Good luck!

KEY TERMS AND DEFINITIONS

18 U.S.C.S 3583 (E) (1) - Statute that permits the Court to terminate a term of supervised release after a defendant serves one year on supervised release.

COMMUTATION - A reduction of sentence granted by the U.S. President to correct injustice that has occurred in the criminal justice process.

COMPASSIONATE RELEASE - A reduction of sentence granted by an inmate's sentencing Court by motion of the Director of the BOP under extraordinary and compelling circumstances, in accordance with 18 U.S.C.S 3582.

EXECUTIVE CLEMENCY - The power of the U.S. President to grant an offender a pardon, commutation or reprieve of his or her sentence.

FURLOUGH - An authorized absence from an institution by an inmate who is not under escort of a BOP staff member, U.S. Marshal, State or Federal Agent.

GOOD CONDUCT TIME (GCT) - The amount of time credited to an inmate for sentences over one year.

HALFWAY HOUSE - (See Residential Re-entry Center - RRC) A community transitional home, operated under the BOP, where inmates spend up to a year from their release transitioning back into society.

CHAPTER 13: THE BEGINNING OF THE END!

HALFWAY HOUSE PACKAGE - A package prepared by the Case Manager 18 months prior to the release of an inmate, which is presented to U.S. Probation and the RRM to determine the inmate's re-entry needs and the date he or she will be released from prison, go to home confinement or be placed in a RRC.

MERRY-GO-ROUND - The process where inmates go around to several departments the day before their release to gain signatures that show they are in compliance and ready for release.

PARDON - An executive act of grace given to an offender by the U.S. President that is a symbol of forgiveness. A pardon restores civil rights and facilitates the restoration of professional and other licenses that may have been lost by reason of a conviction.

RELEASE PREPARATION PROGRAM (RPP) - A series of workshops offered in all BOP institutions and required for inmates to be considered for RRC placement or home confinement.

RELOCATION PACKAGE - A package prepared by the Case Manager when an inmate requests to change their address outside of their sentencing District. This package must be approved by the U.S. Probation office in the relocation District.

REPRIEVE - A suspension of execution of a sentence for a period of time granted by the U.S. President.

RESIDENTIAL DRUG ABUSE TREATMENT PROGRAM (RDAP) - An intensive drug abuse treatment offered to inmates who have been diagnosed with a drug abuse disorder. Participation in this 500-hour course can grant inmates up to 12 months off their sentence.

RESIDENTIAL RE-ENTRY CENTER (RRC) - A community transitional home, operated under the BOP, where inmates spend up to a year from their release transitioning back into society; Also known as a "Halfway House."

RESIDENTIAL RE-ENTRY MANAGER (RRM) - The manager who supervises the RRC.

SECOND CHANCE ACT - A law signed into effect by former U.S. President George W. Bush, that gives allowances for re-entry services for inmates. In this provision, inmates can obtain up to 12 months in a RRC to help them transition successfully back into society.

SENTENCING REFORM ACT OF 1984 (SRA) - A law that went into effect on November 1, 1987 which abolished federal parole and reduced good time for Federal inmates.

AFTERWORD

The U.S. is in the middle of a boom! Contrary to what you may have read, more women are being incarcerated than ever before in history. First time, non-violent offenders are finding themselves behind bars for acts that would not have been considered criminal 10 years ago. This might be the situation you're facing right now. It doesn't seem fair, but it's the new reality. Orange is definitely the new black!

I sincerely hope this guidebook has helped ease your mind and prepared you to enter the Federal prison system. At the very least, you can now focus on the important things in your life such as your family, your health and your piece of mind. Everything else is in the book.

You will be challenged during your indictment, sentencing and imprisonment, in ways you never imagined. How you deal with it is up to you. It's been said that character is not formed during difficult times, it is revealed. Allow your character to be revealed. Cherish the family and friends who have supported you throughout your life, especially during these adverse times. Your attitude will predict your future, so be sure to look at the positive side of everything.

Establish a routine in prison and look forward to the "little" things each day like television shows, phone calls, mail and email. I talked to my son every other day while in prison and many times that was the highlight of my day. Some days, that's all you need. But, when you need more, I suggest you find yourself a mentor before you enter BOP custody; someone you can call, write or email whenever you need their strength to help you get through another day.

The Chaplain advised us to write down, at the end of each day, five positive things that happened to us that day. He said some days it might be difficult, but there would always be five things you could recall that were positive from the day. He was right! A positive thought might come from something as simple as hearing your favorite song on the radio or something more complex like knitting a blanket. Whatever works for you!

I won't tell you it's been easy navigating through the Federal prison system, but I can assure you that you definitely have an advantage. You've been pro-active and armed yourself for the battle by absorbing the information contained in this book. You're ready!

Just like the ladies who contributed to this book, I too, advise you to KEEP BUSY! Use the information in Chapter 8 to find a prison job that you enjoy, volunteer to teach or enroll in a class, keep yourself healthy through daily exercise. Do whatever it takes to keep your mind and body busy. Ask yourself every day, "What have I done to better myself today?" If you can't think of one thing from that day, vow to do something the next day. It can be as simple as reading a self help book or enrolling in an ACE class, but DO IT! You are preparing yourself for your re-entry with every action you take behind bars. Be wise, be cautious and soon you will once again be free!

BIBLIOGRAPHY

Belanger, L. Powell. *The Prisoner's Guide to Survival.* Washington: PSI Publishing, Inc., 2000.

Richards, Jonathan. *Federal Prison: A Comprehensive Survival Guide.* California: SK Enterprises, 2012.

U.S. Department of Justice, FBOP. *Inmate Admission & Orientation Handbook.* April 1, 2014.

Taylor, Jon Marc. *Prisoners Guerrilla Handbook To Correspondence Programs In The United States & Canada.* Washington: Prison Legal News, 2009.

ABOUT THE AUTHOR

Lisa Barrett, born and raised in Scranton, Pennsylvania is an educator and prison reform activist who holds a Masters Degree in Education from Wilkes University in Wilkes-Barre, Pennsylvania.

For nearly 30 years, Barrett taught in the Pennsylvania public school system and advocated for education reform as a local Teacher's Association President and Regional Director of Political Action for the State Teacher's Association.

In 2013 Barrett was indicted on Federal charges for theft and embezzlement of labor union funds and sentenced to serve a year in Federal prison. Behind bars, Barrett developed a passion to educate and assist incarcerated individuals, which inspired her to write "How To Navigate Through Federal Prison And Gain An Early Release."

Barrett currently resides in Shavertown, Pennsylvania with her son JD. Today she is utilizing her experience as an educator, political activist and an overcomer to create awareness about the lengthy sentences of incarcerated women, make strides for prison reform and educate women behind bars.

GLOSSARY

18 U.S.C.S 3583 (E) (1) - Statute that permits the Court to terminate a term of supervised release after a defendant serves one year on supervised release.

2241 MOTION - A Motion in accordance with 28 U.S.C.S 2241 that prisoners can utilize to challenge: (1) an improper revocation of probation, (2) the computation of a sentence, (3) the revocation of sentencing credits, (4) how a sentence is being imposed or (5) challenge the denial of bail.

2255 MOTION - A Motion in accordance with 28 U.S.C.S 2255 seeking to vacate, set aside or correct the sentence of a prisoner filed within 12 months from the time he or she was sentenced, or 15 months from the denial of his or her direct appeal.

3582 MOTION - A Motion to the Courts to reduce a prisoner's sentence based on new sentencing guideline ranges imposed by the Sentencing Commission, in accordance with 18 U.S.C.S 3582.

ADMISSIONS & ORIENTATION (A&O) - New inmate orientation process. All new inmates are placed on A&O status until they complete the A&O program, which includes a presentation introducing the prison staff and policies of the institution.

ADULT CONTINUING EDUCATION (ACE) - Educational classes offered at most BOP institutions often taught by inmates. Sentry credit is awarded upon successful completion of an ACE class.

APPRENTICESHIP - A program sponsored by the U.S. Department of Labor providing inmates with on-the-job training and education in specialized fields.

ASSOCIATE WARDEN (AW) - The individual who assists the Warden with day to day duties ensuring the security of the institution. In larger facilities there may be more than one AW.

BOP PROGRAM POLICY STATEMENT - The set rules and procedures that govern the operations of the BOP.

BP-8.5 - The first step in the informal resolution process where an inmate lodges a complaint to the direct staff member or department where the problem occurred.

BP-9 - The first step in the Administrative Remedy process where an inmate appeals the decision of staff to the Warden.

BP-10 - The second step in the Administrative Remedy process where an inmate appeals the decision of the Warden to the Regional Director.

BP-11 - The third step in the Administrative Remedy process where an inmate appeals the Regional Director's decision to the Central Office/General Counsel.

BP-199 - The form inmates complete to send money out from their Commissary account to a recipient of their choice.

BP-230 - The appeal request form used to challenge a DHO ruling, which goes to the BOP Regional Director.

BP-231 - The appeal request form used to challenge the BOP Regional Director's response regarding a DHO ruling, which goes to the Central Office/General Counsel.

BUNKIE - An inmate's cell mate that is housed in the same immediate area. Generally, bunkies share the same bunk bed.

BUREAU OF PRISONS (BOP) - A division of the U.S. Department of Justice responsible for the administration of the Federal prison system.

CAPTAIN - The individual in charge of all prison guards who supervises and maintains control over the security of the institution.

CALL OUT - The computerized listing of appointments for inmates that can be checked daily through TRULINCS. Also known as Change Sheet.

CAMP ADMINISTRATOR - (See Unit Manager) The person responsible for security and general operations of a Camp (FPC).

CAPTAIN - The individual in charge of all the prison guards who supervises and maintains control over the security of the institution.

CAREER RESOURCE CENTER (CRC) - A designated area open to inmates at most BOP institutions where educational, career and re-entry resources are available for use.

CASE MANAGER - (See Unit Case Manager) The staff person responsible for all casework services and other documentation relating to an inmate's commitment such as classification material, progress reports, release plans, transfers and Financial Responsibility Program payments. The Case Manager serves as a liaison with the administration, Residential Re-entry Center personnel and other criminal justice authorities. The Case Manager conducts team meetings where an inmate is supplied release information and is assisted with plans for release.

CHANGE OUT - The process where inmates exchange the clothes they initially receive at R&D for official standard prison uniforms, T-shirts and undergarments. Also known as "Dress Out."

CHANGE SHEET - The daily computerized listing of changes that affect inmates such as job changes.

CHOW HALL - The lunch room inmates eat in, also referred to as the "Dining Hall."

COMMISSARY - The BOP store inmates shop at during designated days and times.

COMMON FARE - Special trays prepared for Muslim or Jewish inmates that meet Halal/Kosher standards.

COMMUTATION - A reduction of sentence granted by the U.S. President to correct injustice that has occurred in the criminal justice process.

COMPASSIONATE RELEASE - A reduction of sentence granted by an inmate's sentencing Court by motion of the Director of the BOP under extraordinary and compelling circumstances, in accordance with 18 U.S.C.S 3582.

COMPOUND - The grounds of the prison facility.

COMPOUND CLEANING SERVICE (CCS) - The maintenance of the prison grounds, landscaping and trash pick up jobs in higher security institutions.

CONSTRUCTION MAINTENANCE SERVICE (CMS) - Construction, Maintenance, Electric, Paint, Plumbing, Safety, Woodworking, Welding and HVAC shops in minimum security facilities.

CONTRABAND - Items not allowed in a BOP facility including all items inmates were not authorized to bring into the facility, are not able to purchase on Commissary and modified items. Items taken out of a designated work area or from Food Service are also considered contraband.

COP OUT - The form completed by an inmate to make a request of staff. Officially called a BPA-148

CORRECTIONAL OFFICER (CO) - Refers to the prison guards or officers who guard the prison facility. They are usually dressed in white or blue shirts with their names embroidered on the left side and blue khaki pants. These individuals can be called upon if you have security issues or general questions about the functions of the facility.

CORRESPONDENCE COURSES - Courses that can be taken through the mail that do not require Internet access. Correspondence courses vary from certificate programs to degree programs.

CORRLINKS - The Internet company that manages all inmate public messages (email). The company's official website is www.corrlinks.com.

COUNSELOR - (See Unit Counselor) The staff person who provides counseling and guidance for inmates in terms of adjusting to prison. He or she is the individual to approach with personal difficulties. The Counselor regularly assists in resolving day to day problems, approves visitors and assists with attorney calls. He or she is typically the first person you will meet during intake and will assist you with your telephone and email set up.

COUNT - The process of physically counting inmates in their housing area, which occurs at least 5 times daily. Stand up counts require the inmate to silently stand in their cell/cube while being counted.

DESIGNATION AND SENTENCE COMPUTATION CENTER (DSCC) - A division of the BOP, located in Grand Prairie, Texas that designates offenders to a specific prison and performs sentence computation to calculate sentence length and release date.

DETAINER - A hold on an inmate for unresolved warrants or pending charges.

DIRECT APPEAL - An Appeal of the District Court's ruling to the Court of Appeals.

DISCIPLINARY HEARING OFFICER (DHO) - An officer who presides over disciplinary hearings on all Greatest and High severity prohibited acts and other violations referred by the Unit Disciplinary Committee (UDC).

DISTANCE EDUCATION TRAINING COUNCIL (DETC) - An accreditation council recognized by Government, private work force and other civil service industries.

DRUG ABUSE EDUCATION COURSE (DAEC) - A mandatory program offered at all BOP facilities for inmates who have a history of drug use.

ELECTROCARDIOGRAM (EKG) - A screening administered to new inmates and annually to other inmates, which assesses the condition of the heart.

ENGLISH AS A SECOND LANGUAGE (ESL) - A mandatory program for non-English speaking inmates scoring below an 8th grade level in English proficiency.

EXECUTIVE CLEMENCY - The power of the U.S. President to grant an offender a pardon, commutation or reprieve of his or her sentence.

EXPLOSIVE DETECTION CANINES (EDC) - Also known as the 'Puppies Behind Bars' program where dogs are trained to detect explosives for the the U.S. Government.

FEDERAL PRISON INDUSTRY (FPI) - (See UNICOR) A wholly owned subsidiary of the U.S. Government that runs factories and service centers at many Federal prisons, employing Federal inmates.

FINANCIAL RESPONSIBILITY PROGRAM (FRP) - (See also Inmate Financial Responsibility Program) A systematic inmate payment program for court-ordered restitution, fines, fees and court costs.

FOREMAN - The direct supervisor of inmates for a particular department within a facility.

FURLOUGH - An authorized absence from an institution by an inmate who is not under escort of a BOP staff member, U.S. Marshal, State or Federal Agent.

GENERAL EQUIVALENCY DIPLOMA (GED) - A mandatory credential program for inmates who have not earned a high school diploma.

GOOD CONDUCT TIME (GCT) - The amount of time credited to an inmate for sentences over one year.

HALFWAY HOUSE - (See Residential Re-entry Center - RRC) A community transitional home, operated under the BOP, where inmates spend up to a year from their release transitioning back into society.

HALFWAY HOUSE PACKAGE - A package prepared by the Case Manager 18 months prior to the release of an inmate, which is presented to U.S. Probation and the RRM to determine the inmate's re-entry needs and the date he or she will be released from prison, go to home confinement or be placed in a RRC.

IDLE - A written disability excuse, issued through the Health Services Department, from work and other activities for up to 3 days of absence.

INCIDENT REPORT - Also referred to as a "shot." A formal report written against an inmate who violates BOP rules.

INMATE FINANCIAL RESPONSIBILITY PROGRAM - (See also Financial Responsibility Program - FRP) A systematic inmate payment program for court-ordered restitution, fines, fees and costs.

INMATE PERFORMANCE PAY (IPP) - The four levels of pay that inmates receive from grade one through four, which is based on inmate performance.

INMATE TELEPHONE SYSTEM (ITS) - The account used by inmates for telephone use within the BOP.

INTAKE SCREENING - The process that is undertaken when a new inmate enters a facility, which includes being photographed, fingerprinted and strip-searched. It also includes a medical screening and psychological interview.

INTERSTATE AGREEMENT DETAINER ACT (IADA) - A contract between 48 states (excluding Mississippi and Louisiana), the Federal Government and the District of Columbia, where an inmate must expeditiously be sent to face trial on a pending matter upon his or her demand, prior to the termination of their sentence in another state or jurisdiction.

JUDGMENT AND COMMITMENT ORDER (J&C) - The J&C is also referred to as the Judgment or Judgment Order. It is the court-issued document that stipulates the duration of the sentence, monetary penalty amount, if any, and conditions of release. A copy of the J&C can be obtained from the Case Manager.

LIEUTENANT (LT) - A higher ranking CO who supervises prison guards. If a problem occurs that the assigned prison guard is unable to handle, inmates can request to see the LT in charge. When an inmate is causing a problem, the CO will frequently call an LT to oversee disciplinary actions.

LOCK BOX - The location where money orders and checks are received for all BOP inmates.

MAILBOX RULE - The Federal Court rule that deems legal mail filed by an inmate when it is handed to and logged in by a prison staff member.

GLOSSARY

MAINTENANCE PAY - The minimum pay an inmate can receive for his or her services. Currently the rate is $5.25 per month.

MANAGEMENT VARIABLE (MGTV) - A variable used in determining inmate placement in higher security Federal facilities regardless of the points the individual has.

MERRY-GO-ROUND - The process where inmates go around to several departments the day before their release to gain signatures that show they are in compliance and ready for release.

MOTHERS INFANTS NURTURING TOGETHER (MINT) PROGRAM - A 3-6 month program available to women who are pregnant and incarcerated in the Federal prison system. Non-residential MINT programs are operated through RRCs. The 12 month, residential MINT program is offered at one BOP facility in West Virginia.

NATIONAL MENU - The menu followed in most every institution within the BOP. Meals are standardized based on this menu.

OUT OF BOUNDS - A BOP infraction for inmates who are not in their properly designated area at a particular time.

OVER THE COUNTER MEDICATION (OTC) - Non-prescription medications such as ibuprofen, eye drops, and allergy medicines available for purchase from Commissary.

PAC (PHONE ACCESS CODE) AND PIN NUMBER - The numbers assigned to inmates by the BOP that allows access to phone, email and Commissary accounts.

PARDON - An executive act of grace given to an offender by the U.S. President that is a symbol of forgiveness. A pardon restores civil rights and facilitates the restoration of professional and other licenses that may have been lost by reason of a conviction.

PILL LINE - The daily issuance of restricted medications by a Medical Staff officer where inmates form a line for individual, supervised distribution.

PRE-SENTENCE REPORT (PSR) - Also known as the Pre-Sentence Investigative Report (PSI). A report prepared by the U.S. Probation Department prior to an offender's sentencing that includes personal history and the details of the offense committed, among other important information. The PSR is heavily utilized by the Judge, BOP, U.S. Probation and prison staff.

PRE-RELEASE ACCOUNT - An account inmates may set up through TRULINCS where money can be transferred and saved for release.

PRO SE - The act of an inmate filing a motion without the assistance of an attorney. The inmate may NOT have an attorney of record.

RECALL - The process of inmates being called to their housing units at a particular time, usually in preparation for count.

RECEIVING AND DISCHARGE (R&D) - The area where inmates both enter a Federal facility and exit upon release. It is also the designated area where intake screening takes place.

REFUSAL STATUS - The status of an inmate who fails to meet their financial obligation for monthly or quarterly repayment of restitution, fines, fees and costs.

REGISTRATION NUMBER - The 8-digit identification number assigned to each inmate by the U.S. Marshal Service. It is the number that is printed on the inmate's identification which is included on all inmate documentation or correspondence, including mail.

RELEASE PREPARATION PROGRAM (RPP) - A series of workshops offered in all BOP institutions and required for inmates to be considered for RRC placement or home confinement.

RELOCATION PACKAGE - A package prepared by the Case Manager when an inmate requests to change their address outside of their sentencing District. This package must be approved by the U.S. Probation office in the relocation District.

REPRIEVE - A suspension of execution of a sentence for a period of time granted by the U.S. President.

RESIDENTIAL DRUG ABUSE TREATMENT PROGRAM (RDAP) - An intensive drug abuse treatment offered to inmates who have been diagnosed with a drug abuse disorder. Participation in this 500-hour course can grant inmates up to 12 months off their sentence.

RESIDENTIAL RE-ENTRY CENTER (RRC) - (See Halfway House) A community transitional home, operated under the BOP, where inmates spend up to a year from their release transitioning back into society.

RESIDENTIAL RE-ENTRY MANAGER (RRM) - The manager who supervises the RRC.

RESOLVE PROGRAM - A BOP non-residential program offered to inmates who have a history of physical or sexual abuse.

RULE 35 MOTION - A motion from the Government, after sentencing, seeking to reduce a defendant's sentence for his or her cooperation with the Government.

SECOND CHANCE ACT - A law signed into effect by former U.S. President George W. Bush, that gives allowances for re-entry services for inmates. In this provision, inmates can obtain up to 12 months in a RRC to help them transition successfully back into society.

SENTENCING REFORM ACT OF 1984 (SRA) - A law that went into effect on November 1, 1987 which abolished Federal parole and reduced good time for Federal inmates.

SENTRY - The BOP computer database that keeps track of information about the security level of inmates, which directly affects the offender's custody level based on a variety of factors including: voluntary surrender eligibility, severity of offense, criminal history score, history of violence or escape attempts, detainers, age, education and substance abuse history.

SENTRY CREDIT - Credit given to inmates for participation in certain Recreation and Education classes. These credits help reduce the security levels of inmate participants.

SEX OFFENDER MANAGEMENT PROGRAM (SOMP) - A voluntary sex offender program offered at certain federal facilities.

SHAKEDOWN - When BOP staff or officers search a particular area.

SHOT - An inmate term for incident report.

SKILLS PROGRAM - A residential treatment program to help inmates with intellectual and emotional difficulties adjust to institutional living.

SNITCH - An inmate that cooperates with the Government or informs prison officials of the improper behavior of other inmates.

SPECIAL HOUSING UNIT (SHU) - Also referred to as the 'hole.' An undesirable, segregated area of the prison where inmates serve time on disciplinary sanctions.

SPECIAL MAIL - Mail from the U.S. Courts (Including U.S. Probation, an attorney and Government official, including Congressional members and the President of the United States) which may not be read by BOP staff. Special mail must be opened in the presence of the inmate recipient.

SPECIAL PURCHASE ORDER (SPO) - Special orders placed by inmates for items not available on Commissary such as craft items and religious articles.

THRESHOLD PROGRAM - A 6-month spirituality based program offered in the BOP through Chaplaincy Services.

TOWN DRIVER - An inmate driver position with the responsibility of running errands for prison officials and transporting low security inmates outside of the facility.

TRUFONE - The phone service for inmates in BOP custody, which can be utilized for inmate personal use.

TRULINCS - The Trust Fund Limited Inmate Computer System (TRULINCS) allows inmates to access multiple services including: Account Transactions, Bulletin Board, Contact List, Law Library, Manage Funds, Manage TRU-Units, Prescription Refill, Print, Public Messaging (email), Request to Staff and Survey.

UNICOR - (See Federal Prison Industries - FPI) A wholly owned subsidiary of the U.S. Government that runs factories and service centers at many Federal prisons, which employs Federal inmates.

UNIT CASE MANAGER - (See Case Manager) The staff person responsible for all casework services and other documentation relating to an inmate's commitment such as classification material, progress reports, release plans, transfers and Financial Responsibility Program payments. The Case Manager serves as a liaison with the administration, Residential Re-entry Center personnel and criminal justice authorities. The Case Manager conducts team meetings where an inmate is supplied release information and is assisted with plans for release.

UNIT COUNSELOR - (See Counselor) The staff person who provides counseling and guidance for inmates in terms of adjusting to prison. He or she is the individual to approach with personal difficulties. The Counselor regularly assists in resolving day to day problems, approves visitors and assists with attorney calls. He or she is typically the first person you will meet during intake and will assist you with your telephone and email set up.

UNIT DISCIPLINARY COMMITTEE (UDC) - A committee of Unit Team members who preside over disciplinary hearings and make findings on Moderate and Low severity level offenses.

UNIT MANAGER - (See Camp Administrator) The person responsible for security and general operations of a BOP facility.

U.S. SENTENCING GUIDELINES - Guidelines set by the U.S. Sentencing Commission that help Judges determine the sentencing range for offenders based on their offense.

WARDEN - The individual who holds the highest position over all institution staff and oversees the operation of the entire institution. He or she must sign off on all major decisions rendered throughout the institution.

WOMEN INFANTS CHILDREN (WIC) - A program offering dairy products and other groceries free of charge to women, infants and children in need.

Resources

RESIDENTIAL RE-ENTRY MANAGEMENT (RRM)

FIELD OFFICES

RRM Atlanta
Residential Reentry Office
719 McDonough Blvd SE
Atlanta, GA 30315
Email: CAT/CCM@bop.gov
Phone: 404-635-5679
Fax: 404-635-5240

RRM Baltimore
Residential Reentry Office
302 Sentinel Drive, Suite 200
Annapolis Junction, MD 20701
Email: CBR/CCM@bop.gov
Phone: 301-317-3142
Fax: 301-317-3138

RRM Chicago
Residential Reentry Office
200 W Adams Street, Room 2915
Chicago, IL 60606
Email: CCH/CCM@bop.gov
Phone: 312-886-2317
Fax: 312-886-2118

RRM Cincinnati
Residential Reentry Office
36 E 7th Street, Suite 2107-A
Cincinnati, OH 45202
Email: CCN/CCM @bop.gov
Phone: 513-684-2603
Fax: 513-684-2590

RRM Dallas
Residential Reentry Office
US Armed Forces Reserve CMPL
344 Marine Forces Drive
Grand Prairie, TX 75051
Email: CDA/CCM@bop.gov
Phone: 972-730-8837
Fax: 972-730-8838

RRM Denver
Residential Reentry Office
9595 W Quincy Ave
Littleton, CO 80123
Email: CDE/CCM@bop.gov
Phone: 303-980-2373
Fax: 303-980-2374

RRM Detroit
Residential Reentry Office
4026 E Arkona Road
Milan, MI 48160
Email: CDT/CCM@bop.gov
Phone: 734-439-7653
Fax: 734-439-7671

RRM Houston
Residential Reentry Office
515 Rusk Avenue, Room 12102
Houston, TX 77002
Email: CHN/CCM@bop.gov
Phone: 713-718-4781
Fax: 713-718-4680

RRM Kansas City
Residential Reentry Office
400 State Avenue, Room 131
Kansas City, KS 66101
Email: CKC/CCM@bop.gov
Phone: 913-551-1117
Fax: 913-551-1120

RRM Long Beach
Residential Reentry Office
PO Box 323
San Pedro, CA 90733
Email: CLB/CCM@bop.gov
Phone: 310-732-5179
Fax: 310-732-5291

RRM Miami
Residential Reentry Office
401 N Miami Avenue
Miami, FL 33128
Email: CMM/CCM@bop.gov
Phone: 305-536-5710
Fax: 305-536-4024

RRM Minneapolis
Residential Reentry Office
300 South 4th Street, Suite 1210

Minneapolis, MN 55415
Email: CMS/CCM@bop.gov
Phone: 612-332-5030
Fax: 612-332-5029

RRM Montgomery
Residential Reentry Office
Maxwell AFB, Bldg 1209
820 Willow Street
Montgomery, AL 36112
Email: CMY/CCM@bop.gov
Phone: 334-293-2360
Fax: 334-293-2357

RRM Nashville
Residential Reentry Office
701 Broadway Street, Suite 124
Nashville, TN 37203
Email: CNV/CCM@bop.gov
Phone: 615-736-5148
Fax: 615-736-5147

RRM New York
Residential Reentry Office
PO Box 329014
Brooklyn, NY 11232
Email: CNK/CCM@bop.gov
Phone: 718-840-4219
Fax: 718-840-4207

RESOURCES

RRM Orlando
Residential Reentry Office
6303 County Road 500
Wildwood, FL 34785
Email: COR/CCM@bop.gov
Phone: 352-689-7390
Fax: 352-689-7396

RRM Philadelphia
Residential Reentry Office
2nd & Chestnut Streets - 7th Floor
Philadelphia, PA 19106
Email: CPA/CCM@bop.gov
Phone: 215-521-7300
Fax: 215-521-7486

RRM Phoenix
Residential Reentry Office
230 N First Avenue, Suite 405
Phoenix, AZ 85003
Email: CPH/CCM@bop.gov
Phone: 602-514-7075
Fax: 602-514-7076

RRM Pittsburgh
Residential Reentry Office
1000 Liberty Avenue, Suite 1315
Pittsburgh, PA 15222
Email: CPG/CCM@bop.gov
Phone: 412-395-4740
Fax: 412-395-4730

RRM Raleigh
Residential Reentry Office
PO Box 7000
Butner, NC 27509
Email: CRL/CCM@bop.gov
Phone: 919-575-2080
Fax: 919-575-2073

RRM Sacramento
Residential Reentry Office
501 I Street, Suite 9-400
Sacramento, CA 95814
Email: CSC/CCM@bop.gov
Phone: 916-930-2010
Fax: 916-930-2008

RRM Salt Lake City
Residential Reentry Office
324 South State Street, Suite 228
Salt Lake City, UT 84111
Email: CSL/CCM@bop.gov
Phone: 801-524-4212
Fax: 801-524-3112

RRM San Antonio
Residential Reentry Office
727 East Cesar E Chavez Blvd
Suite B-138
San Antonio, TX 78206
Email: CSA/CCM@bop.gov
Phone: 210-472-6225
Fax: 210-472-6224

RRM Seattle
Residential Reentry Office
PO Box 13901
Seattle, WA 98198
Email: CSE/CCM@bop.gov
Phone: 206-870-1011
Fax: 206-870-1012

RRM St. Louis
Residential Reentry Office
1222 Spruce Street
St. Louis, MO 63101
Email: CST/CCM@bop.gov
Phone: 314-539-2376
Fax: 314-539-2465

RRM Washington, DC
Residential Reentry Office
302 Sentinel Drive
Suite 200
Annapolis Junction, MD 20701
Email: CBR/CCM@bop.gov
Fax: 301-317-3142

National Organizations

RESOURCES FOR INMATES

ACLU – American Civil Liberties Union
125 Broad Street
18th Floor
New York, NY 10004
212-549-2500
www.aclu.org

National organization devoted to promoting and protecting the civil rights of all Americans including First Amendment rights, equal protection under the law, due process and privacy. Affiliate state services.

ACLU National Prison Project
915 15th Street N.W., 7th Floor
Washington, DC 20005
202-393-4930
www.aclu.org/prisons

Assists with class action suits involving prison conditions and related issues in Federal and state institutions. Also provides advice and materials to individuals or organizations involved in prison issues. Does not handle cases on an individual basis or post-conviction cases.

AFSC – American Friends Service Committee
Criminal Justice Program
1501 Cherry Street
Philadelphia, PA 19102
215-241-7130
www.afsc.org

Advocates criminal justice reform and provides information and referrals to inmates and their families.

The Aleph Institute
9540 Collins Avenue
Surfside, FL 33154
305-864-5553
www.aleph-institute.org

Implements a host of programs for Jewish inmates who are isolated due to incarceration.

Center for Children of Incarcerated Parents
714 W California Boulevard
Pasadena, CA 91105
626-397-1396
www.e-ccip.org

Devoted to the development of model services for children of criminal offenders and their families. Offers free publication each month, an online journal and program information.

Families Against Mandatory Minimums (FAMM)
1612 K Street, NW Suite 1400
Washington, DC 20006
202-822-6700
www.famm.org

A national organization of citizens working to reform mandatory minimum sentencing laws for nonviolent offenses. Publishes a quarterly newsletter.

FedCURE
P.O. Box 15667
Plantation, FL 33318-5667
www.fedcure.org

Advocacy on behalf of the federal inmate population is the central focus of FedCURE. Enlightening society about federal prison reality, FedCURE seeks to create a paradigm where elected officials and American society have a clear understanding of the issues confronted by the federal inmate population.

International Prison Ministry
P.O. Box 2868
Costa Mesa, CA 92628
800-527-1212
www.chaplainray.com

Freely distributes Bibles and Christian literature to inmates. Letters from prisoners are read and prayerfully answered. Different books are sent every time an inmate corresponds with IPM.

Prisoner Visitation and Support (PVS)
1501 Cherry Street
Philadelphia, PA 19102
215-241-7117
www.prisonervisitation.org

Prisoner Visitation and Support (PVS) is a volunteer visitation program to Federal and Military prisoners throughout the United States with priority given to inmates who do not ordinarily receive visits from family and friends. Their purpose is to provide prisoners with regular, face-to-face, contact from the world outside of prison to help them cope with prison life and prepare for a successful re-entry into society.

Volunteers of America
1660 Duke Street
Alexandria, VA 22314
703-341-5000
www.voa.org

Helps those in need to rebuild lives by providing emergency services and resources to ex-offenders and their families. Services include employment training, technical assistance, clothing, tools and food.

BOP Contact Offices

U.S. Department of Justice
Office of the Inspector General
950 Pennsylvania Avenue, NW Suite 4322
Washington, DC 20530-0001
202-514-3435

Central Office
Federal Bureau of Prisons
320 First Street, NW
Washington, DC 20534
202-307-3198

Mid-Atlantic Regional Office
302 Sentinel Drive, Suite 200
Annapolis Junction, MD 20701
301-317-3100

North Central Regional Office
Gateway Complex Tower II, 8th Floor
400 State Avenue
Kansas City, KS 66101-2492
913-621-3939

Northeast Regional Office
U.S. Customs House, 7th Floor
2nd and Chestnut Streets
Philadelphia, PA 19106
215-521-7300

South Central Regional Office
4211 Cedar Springs Road, Suite 300
Dallas, TX 72519
972-730-8600

Southeast Regional Office
3800 North Camp Creek Parkway, SW
Building 2000
Atlanta, GA 30331-5099
678-686-1200

Western Regional Office
7950 Dublin Boulevard, 3rd Floor
Dublin, CA 94568
209-956-9700

Index

Symbols

2241 Motion 129
2255 Motion 133
3582 Motion 134

A

Adult Continuing Education (ACE) 93
Apprenticeship 95, 118, 152

B

BOP Program Policy Statement 127
BP-8.5 127
BP-9 128, 129
BP-10 128, 129
BP-11 129
BP-199 71, 77, 81
BP-230 131
BP-231 131
Bunkie 41, 150
Bureau of Prisons (BOP) 9, 17

C

Camp Administrator 146
Case Manager 66, 159, 168, 169
Change Sheet 47
Commissary 47, 66, 68, 69, 71, 72, 77, 78, 79, 81, 84
Common Fare 84
Commutation 165
Compassionate release 166
Compassionate Release 166, 167
Compound 31, 39, 41, 125, 142, 146, 154, 156
Contraband 28, 47, 48, 65

Cop Out 35, 75, 84, 92, 110, 111, 112, 114, 116, 127, 167, 170
Correctional Officer (CO) 26
Corrlinks 36, 37, 70, 73, 103
Counselor 36
Count 41, 46, 145

D

Designation and Sentence Computation Center (DSCC 17
Direct Appeal 133
Disciplinary Hearing Officer (DHO) 129
Drug Abuse Education Course (DAEC) 114

E

English as a Second Language (ESL) 117
Executive Clemency 165
Explosive Detection Canines (EDC) 152

F

Financial Responsibility Program (FRP) 20, 23
Foreman 39, 92, 96
Furlough 97, 146, 152, 159, 160, 161

G

General Equivalency Diploma (GED) 117
Good Conduct Time (GCT) 162

H

Halfway House 131, 162, 164, 168, 169
Halfway House Package 168

I

Idle 48, 110
Incident Report 47, 48, 118, 129
Inmate Performance Pay (IPP) 91
Inmate Telephone System (ITS) 66
Interstate Agreement Detainer Act (IADA) 132

L

Lieutenant (LT) 42, 156

M

Mailbox Rule 132
Maintenance Pay 96, 97, 114
Management Variable (MGTV) 19
Merry-Go-Round 169

N

National Menu 83

O

Out of Bounds 48
Over the Counter Medication (OTC) 77

P

PAC (Phone Access Code) and Pin Number 28, 67, 68, 69
Pardon 165
Pill Line 111
Pre-Release Account 71
Pre-Sentence Report (PSR) 17, 74

R

Registration Number 33, 69
Release Preparation Program (RPP) 167
Reprieve 165
Residential Drug Abuse Treatment Program (RDAP) 115
Residential Re-entry Center (RRC) 20, 23, 115, 120, 163, 164
Residential Re-entry Manager (RRM) 168
Resolve Program 113
Rule 35 Motion 134

S

Second Chance Act 164
Sentencing Reform Act of 1984 (SRA) 162
Sentry 18, 100, 116, 151
Sentry Credit 116, 151
Sex Offender Management Program (SOMP) 113
Shakedown 143, 146, 156
Shot 38
Skills Program 113
Snitch 42
Special Housing Unit (SHU) 26, 31
Special Mail 65
Special Purchase Order (SPO) 116

T

Threshold Program 116
Town Driver 154
TRUFONE 66, 67, 68
TRULINCS 36, 37, 38, 47, 63, 67, 69, 70, 72, 73, 77, 81, 111, 119, 126, 127, 170

U

UNICOR 93, 97, 146, 148, 150, 153, 156
Unit Case Manager 20, 23
Unit Counselor 75
Unit Disciplinary Committee (UDC) 129
Unit Manager 21, 23
U.S. Sentencing Guidelines 125

W

Warden 116, 128, 129, 131, 132, 160, 161

Voices International Publications Presents

Voices of
CONSEQUENCES
ENRICHMENT SERIES
CREATED BY: JAMILA T. DAVIS

Unlocking the Prison Doors:
12 Points to Inner Healing
and Restoration

ISBN: 978-09855807-4-2 Textbook
ISBN: 978-09855807-5-9 Workbook/Journal
ISBN: 978-09855807-6-6 Curriculum Guide
is a nondenominational, faith-based instructional manual created to help incarcerated women gain inner healing and restoration. In a comforting voice that readers can recognize and understand, this book provides the tools women need to get past the stage of denial and honestly assess their past behavioral patterns, their criminal conduct and its impact on their lives and others. It provides a platform for women to begin a journey of self-discovery, allowing them to assess the root of their problems and dilemmas and learn how to overcome them.

This book reveals real-life examples and concrete strategies that inspire women to release anger, fear, shame and guilt and embrace a new world of opportunities.

After reading readers will be empowered to release the inner shackles and chains that have been holding them bound and begin to soar in life!

"Changing Lives One Page At A Time."
www.vocseries.com

Voices International Publications Presents

Voices of
CONSEQUENCES
ENRICHMENT SERIES
CREATED BY: JAMILA T. DAVIS

Permission to Dream:
12 Points to Discovering Your Life's Purpose and Recapturing Your Dreams

ISBN: 978-09855807-4-2 Textbook
ISBN: 978-09855807-5-9 Workbook/Journal
ISBN: 978-09855807-6-6 Curriculum Guide

is a nondenominational, faith-based, instruction manual created to inspire incarcerated women to discover their purpose in life and recapture their dreams. In a way readers can identify with and understand, this book provides strategies they can use to overcome the stigma and barriers of being an ex-felon.

This book reveals universal laws and proven self-help techniques that successful people apply in their everyday lives. It helps readers identify and destroy bad habits and criminal thinking patterns, enabling them to erase the defilement of their past.

Step-by-step this book empowers readers to recognize their talents and special skill sets, propelling them to tap into the power of "self" and discover their true potential, and recapture their dreams.

After reading, readers will be equipped with courage and tenacity to take hold of their dreams and become their very best!

"Changing Lives One Page At A Time."
www.vocseries.com

Voices International Publications Presents

Voices of
CONSEQUENCES
ENRICHMENT SERIES
CREATED BY: JAMILA T. DAVIS

Pursuit to A Greater "Self:" 12 Points to Developing Good Character and HealthyRelationships

ISBN: 978-09855807-7-3 Textbook
ISBN: 978-09855807-8-0 Workbook/Journal
ISBN: 978-09855807-9-7 Curriculum Guide

is a non-denominational, faith-based, instruction manual created to help incarcerated women develop good character traits and cultivate healthy relationships.

This book is filled with real-life examples that illustrate how good character traits have helped many people live a more prosperous life, and how deficient character has caused others to fail. These striking examples, along with self-help strategies revealed in this book, are sure to inspire women to dethrone bad character traits and develop inner love, joy, peace, patience, kindness, generosity, faithfulness, gentleness and self-control. This book also instructs women how to utilize these positive character traits to cultivate healthy relationships.

After reading readers will be inspired to let their light shine for the world to see that true reformation is attainable, even after imprisonment!

"Changing Lives One Page At A Time."
www.vocseries.com

NOW AVAILABLE FROM
VOICES
INTERNATIONAL PUBLICATIONS

"Every negative choice we make in life comes with a consequence. Sometimes the costs we are forced to pay are severe!"
— Jamila T. Davis

She's All Caught Up is a real-life cautionary tale that exemplifies the powerful negative influences that affect today's youth and the consequences that arise from poor choices.

Young Jamila grew up in a loving middle class home, raised by two hardworking parents, the Davises, in the suburbs of Jamaica Queens, New York. Determined to afford their children the luxuries that they themselves never had, the Davises provided their children with a good life, hoping to guarantee their children's success.

At first it seemed as though their formula worked. Young Jamila maintained straight As and became her parents ideal "star child," as she graced the stage of Lincoln Center's Avery Fischer Hall in dance recitals and toured the country in a leading role in an off-Broadway play. All was copacetic in the Davis household until high school years when Jamila met her first love Craig- a 16 year old drug dealer from the Southside housing projects of Jamaica Queens.

As this high school teen rebels, breaking loose from her parents' tight reins, the Davises wage an "all-out" battle to save their only daughter whom they love so desperately. But Jamila is in too deep! Poisoned by the thorn of materialism, she lusts after independence, power and notoriety, and she chooses life in the fast lane to claim them.

When this good girl goes bad, it seems there is no turning back! Follow author, Jamila T. Davis (creator of the Voices of Consequences Enrichment Series) in her trailblazing memoir, *She's All Caught Up!*

DECEMBER 2013
ISBN: 978-09855807-3-5
www.voicesbooks.com

NOW AVAILABLE FROM

INTERNATIONAL PUBLICATIONS

"Is it fair that corporate giants get to blame 'small fries' like myself, whom they recruited but they walk away scott-free?"
— Jamila T. Davis

Years before the 2008 Financial Crisis, a major epidemic of mortgage fraud surged throughout the country. The FBI geared up to combat the problem, imprisoning thousands who were alleged to have victimized Wall Street giants, such as Lehman Brothers Bank. Hidden safely behind the auspices of being a "victim," savvy Ivy League bank executives created additional fraudulent schemes to further their profit. Utilizing their "victimizers" as scapegoats, the bankers' clever plan went undetected. Consequently, the real architects of the massive fraudulent lending schemes escaped unpunished. And the "small fries," who the bankers blamed to be the bandits, were left to do big time!

The High Price I Had To Pay is a captivating real-life story that reveals another aspect of the inside fraud perpetrated by Lehman executives that has yet to be told!

This illuminating synopsis by author Jamila T. Davis, who is currently serving a 12 1/2 year sentence in federal prison for bank fraud, is shared from a unique stand point. Davis was labeled by Lehman attorneys as the 25 year old mastermind who devised an elaborate mortgage scheme that defrauded their bank of 22 million dollars. Her shocking story captures the inside tricks of Wall Street elite and takes you up-close and personal into a world driven by greed and power.

Davis' story will leave you amazed and make you think. Have savvy Wall Street executives, such as Richard Fuld, been able to out smart the world? And while these executives escape unpunished, is it fair that "small fries," like Davis, are left to do big time?

Visit www.smashwords.com/books/view/324608
to download your FREE e-book today!
ISBN: 978-09855807-9-7
www.voicesbooks.com

NOW AVAILABLE FROM

VOICES
INTERNATIONAL PUBLICATIONS

"To-date, I have served 16 years of the 30 year sentence that was handed down to me. I feel like I was left here to die, sort of like being buried alive!"
— Michelle Miles

In 1982, during a period when illegal drug use was on the decline, President Ronald Reagan officially announced the War on Drugs. In support of his effort, Congress passed bills to tremendously increase the sentences imposed on drug dealers, including lengthy mandatory minimum sentences. With drug sentences accounting for the majority of the increase, in less than 30 years, the U.S. prison population exploded from 300,000 to more than 2 million! The statistics are well known, but the true faces of those imprisoned and the effects of their incarceration is less publicized.

The High Price I Had To Pay 2, is a captivating real-life story about the life of Michele Miles, a 21 year old, African American woman, who grew up in Marcy Housing Project in Brooklyn, New York. Miles lured in by her boyfriend, Stanley Burrell, tried her hand in the drug game, as a way to escape poverty. Through what she believed to be a promising opportunity, Miles became partners in the notorious "Burrell Organization," which became a thriving enterprise. Overnight, Miles went from "rags-to-riches." In her mind, she was living the life of her dreams.

All was well until the FEDS got wind of the operation. With the help of informants, the Burrell empire swiftly crumbled and the key players were arrested, including Miles. In the end, her role in the drug conspiracy led Miles to receive a thirty year sentence in federal prison.

Miles' story gives readers an inside view of the life of women serving hefty sentences for drug crimes, and the effects of their incarceration. This story will leave you shocked about the rules of prosecution for drug offenders in the U.S. judicial system and make you think. Should a first time, non-violent offender, receive a thirty year sentence?

Visit www.smashwords.com/books/view/377047
to download your FREE e-book today!
ISBN: 978-09911041-0-9
www.voicesbooks.com

NOW AVAILABLE FROM

INTERNATIONAL PUBLICATIONS

"I am a 73 Year Old woman currently serving an 11 year sentence in federal prison. One bad decision landed me a decade plus sentence as a first time, non-violent offender."
— Gwendolyn Hemphill

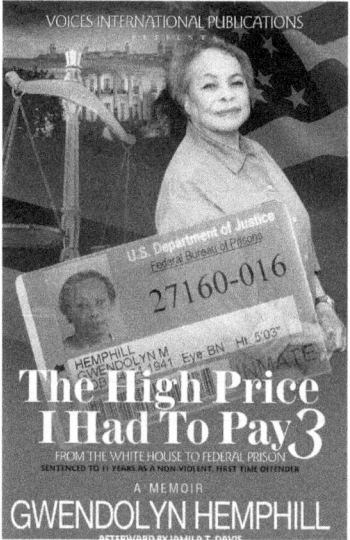

Since 1970, the U.S. prison population has increased seven fold, growing to over 2 million prisoners. Consequently, even though it only consists of 5% of the world's population, America leads the world with the largest prison population. Crime rates are not increasing, yet the U.S. prison population continues to steadily grow. As a result, mass incarceration is a major epidemic that destroys families and costs tax payers billions of dollars each year. The statistics are well known, but the true faces of those imprisoned and the injustices they encounter in the U.S. judicial system is less publicized.

The High Price I Had To Pay, Volume 3, is a captivating true story about the life of Gwendolyn Hemphill, a 73 year old woman currently serving a 11 year sentence for her role in a scheme to defraud the Washington Teachers Union (WTU).

Rising from humble beginnings in the rural town of Johnstown, Pennsylvania, Hemphill worked relentlessly to overcome barriers of poverty and racism. Known for her savvy wit and creative political strategies, she successfully advocated for unions and political groups, including the legendary SNCC, during the era of the civil rights movement. Climbing to the top of the political ladder, as a rising star, Hemphill made her way up to the White House under the Carter Administration. For decades, she vigorously served as a liaison who provided substantial contributions to her community; making waves in the world of Washington D.C. politics. Despite her accomplishments and her stellar career, one bad decision landed Hemphill a decade plus sentence in federal prison, as a first time, non-violent offender.

Hemphill's story gives readers and inside view of the many female, white collar offenders, who are serving lengthy sentences behind bars. This story will leave you questioning is there mercy and equality for all citizens in the U.S. judicial system? And, it will make you think: Should a senior citizen with a stellar past serve a decade plus sentence as a first time, non-violent offender?

Visit www.smashwords.com/books/view/468313
to download your FREE e-book today!
ISBN: 978-0-9911041-2-3
www.voicesbooks.com

ORDER FORM

Mail to: 196-03 Linden Blvd.
St. Albans, NY 11412
or visit us on the web @
www.vocseries.com

QTY	Title	Price
	Unlocking the Prison Doors	14.95
	Unlocking the Prison Doors Workbook/Journal	14.95
	Permission to Dream	14.95
	Permission to Dream Workbook/Journal	14.95
	Pursuit to A Greater "Self"	14.95
	Pursuit to A Greater "Self" Workbook/Journal	14.95
	The High Price I Had To Pay	7.99
	The High Price I Had To Pay 2	7.99
	The High Price I Had To Pay 3	9.99
	How To Navigate Through Federal Prison And Gain An Early Release	39.95
	Total For Books	
	20% Inmate Discount -	
	Shipping/Handling +	
	Total Cost	

* Shipping/Handling 1-3 books 4.95
　　　　　　　4-9 books 8.95
* Incarcerated individuals receive a 20% discount on each book purchase.
* Forms of Accepted Payments: Certified Checks, Institutional Checks and Money Orders.
* Bulk rates are available upon requests for orders of 10 books or more.
* Curriculum Guides are available for group sessions.
* All mail-in orders take 5-7 business days to be delivered. For prison orders, please allow up to (3) three weeks for delivery.

SHIP TO:
Name: _____
Address: _____

_____

_____

City: _____

State: _____ Zip: _____

www.ingramcontent.com/pod-product-compliance
Lightning Source LLC
Chambersburg PA
CBHW052111300426
44116CB00010B/1628